Gavin Souter AO was born in 1929 in Sydney. He joined *The Sydney Morning Herald* in 1947 and worked there for 40 years, serving as a correspondent in New York and London and later as an assistant editor. He is the author of twelve works of non-fiction, including *A Peculiar People* (1968), which won the Foundation of Australian Literary Studies award; *Lion & Kangaroo* (1976), which also won the Foundation of Australian Literary Studies award and was highly commended by the National Book Council for Australian Literature; *Company of Heralds* (1981), which also won the Foundation for Australian Literary Studies award; and *Heralds and Angels* (1992), which won the Victorian Premier's Literary Award. In 1960, Gavin won a Walkley Award; in 1988 he was appointed a Member of the Order of Australia (AM), and raised to Officer level (AO) in 1995; and in 2001 he was awarded the Centenary Medal. He lives in Sydney.

Praise for *Sydney Observed*

'Brilliantly successful.' *The Times Literary Supplement*
'Here, for once, is a description of Sydney which is unblinking but good-mannered, appreciative but unsentimental, factual but not a tourists' guide, opinionated but never eccentric ... a brilliant mosaic.' *The Sydney Morning Herald*

Sydney Observed

Gavin Souter

Illustrated by **George Molnar**

b
BRIO

BRIO

Published in Brio by Xoum in 2017

Xoum Publishing
PO Box Q324, QVB Post Office,
NSW 1230, Australia

www.briobooks.com.au
www.xoum.com.au

First published by Angus & Robertson Ltd in 1965

ISBN 978-1-925143-40-9 (print)
ISBN 978-1-922057-01-3 (digital)

All rights reserved. Without limiting the rights under copyright below, no part of this publication shall be reproduced, stored in or introduced into a retrieval system, or transmitted in any form or by any means (electronic, mechanical, photocopying, recording or otherwise), without the prior permission of both the copyright holder and the publisher.

The moral right of the author has been asserted.

Copyright text © Gavin Souter 1965, 1968, 2017
Copyright illustrations © George Molnar 1968
Cover and internal design and typesetting copyright © Xoum Publishing 2017

Cataloguing-in-publication data is available from the National Library of Australia

Cover design by Xou Creative, www.xoucreative.com.au
Printed and bound in Australia by McPherson's Printing Group

Papers used by Xoum Publishing are natural, recyclable products made from wood grown in sustainable forests. The manufacturing processes conform to the environmental regulations of the country of origin.

AUTHOR'S NOTE

THIS VERSION of *Sydney Observed*, accompanied by the late George Molnar's evocative drawings, was first published in 1968. Since then, of course, Sydney has changed a lot, but not beyond recognition. Arthur Stace has gone to his 'Eternity', and Bea Miles no longer smashes taxi doors or recites Shakespeare in Martin Place. But these and other shades of the city's past survive in memory, which surely means they still belong to Sydney. So here they are again, half a century on.

A few tenses have been altered where necessary and imperial measures are now metric. Otherwise the text is virtually unchanged. Although no attempt has been made to bring it up to date, this younger Sydney differs from the present one surprisingly less than might be expected. In this assertion, I take comfort from Sydney University's Latin motto, which translates as 'The more things change, the more they are the same.'

ARTIST'S NOTE

WHEN I agreed to illustrate this book I had not read it. When I did I realised that Gavin Souter had written a text so evocative that it needed no further visual explanation. So instead of illustrating his text I spread my drawings through the book as embellishments. Any relationship between text and drawings is therefore purely coincidental.

1

THE ONE pleasure Sydney has denied me is that of seeing it for the first time. This is the price of being born here: the city slips gently into one's mind as a murmur of doves, an odour of Moreton Bay figs, a blur of rufous electric trains, and a million other images, until suddenly it is too late: the parts have become whole, but precisely when that fusion took place no one ever knows. There is much to be said for this sort of gradual cognition, yet sometimes – and never more than now – I wish that I could come as a stranger, pass between those yellowish cliffs that reminded Charles Darwin of the Patagonian coast, and discover Sydney all at once. What would I make of it if I came without familiarity, as if from Patagonia?

First I would surely be impressed by its beauty, for Sydney throws itself at anyone who arrives by sea. The only time I ever came home this way, and watched the city unfurl as we steamed slowly up the eastern channel of Port Jackson, the skin on my face began to tingle as it sometimes does when I hear bugles or bagpipes. The harbour was like a wide green strait dividing alien but equally imposing coastlines: on one side the eastern suburbs, all brick and glass and tile from their netted swimming pools to the white lighthouse at Vaucluse and the big water tower above Rose Bay, and on the other side the shores of Mosman, all virgin bush from the cliffs of Middle Head to Taronga Zoo. As we passed Bradley's Head I heard cicadas singing, and they did more to the skin on my face than buglers or pipers ever could.

My next reaction if I came from Patagonia would probably be one of surprise, firstly surprise at the dimensions of the city – the grey mass of the bridge whose arch unites those alien coastlines, the white expanse of the Opera House, and the sprawl of the suburbs whose outer limits can scarcely be seen even from the top of the bridge – and secondly surprise at how the city defies the logic of its location. Sydney exists on the coast of a largely rural continent; it exists on the shores of the southern Pacific Ocean; and geopolitically it exists on the edge of Asia. Thus a stranger might reasonably expect to find an agricultural seaport, British by origin but also Melanesian and Asian by osmosis. He or she would be disappointed, for apart from a few essential economic transactions Sydney pays little heed to its hinterland, and although it now admits more people from other countries than in the past it manages to ignore them pretty successfully, too. Sydney, like most other Australian cities except Darwin, seems curiously out of context – Anglo-Saxon on the edge of Asia, affluent on the edge of poverty, and carefree on the edge of trouble.

No city in the world enjoys itself more than Sydney on a midsummer Saturday afternoon. The weekend crowd sips canned beer thoughtfully at fifty different cricket ovals, plunges its money on the horses at Randwick and Warwick Farm, picnics in the bush, swings back over the gunwhales of five thousand yachts, surfs at Bondi and twenty other beaches, or simply lies on the sand in a half-dream. Surf and sand are never far from Sydney's consciousness, and a stranger casting around for some ready metaphor might well liken the city to one of its myriad beach goers: fair to look upon, but not particularly cerebral; a good sport, but inclined to be complacent and self-indulgent.

Although I am disqualified by long acquaintance from saying how this beach goer would appeal to me at first sight, I can at least look hard at Sydney and try to disown some of the familiarity that blunts perception. The other day I happened to be walking on Turimetta Head – a clifftop far from the city's heart, but very close to mine – and there, half-hidden in coarse brown grass, I noticed for the first time one of those small steel boxes that surveyors call permanent marks. You lift the lid, centre your theodolite over a benchmark inside, and proceed to relate your position to other permanent marks in the distance. In a manner of speaking, this is what I now propose to do with Sydney.

The day I am speaking about was well into summer, but not too warm for sprawling on one's back, listening to the snap of insects, and watching a kestrel ride motionless on a column of soft north-east wind deflected upwards by the cliffs. Now and then the bird's tail and wing feathers would tremble in response to a slight change of wind, and twice it swooped on something tiny in the grass.

By this time of day the surface of the sea has usually heated up sufficiently to release the particles of dust and smoke that have drifted away from Sydney the day before and been compressed overnight in the lower atmosphere. That afternoon, however, the blue of the sky and the deeper blue of the sea were still divided by the stale breath of the city, a long brown band composed of such infinitely varied elements as cigarette smoke, exhaust fumes, coal smoke from Bunnerong and Pyrmont, oil smoke from Kurnell, cremation smoke from Chatswood and Rookwood, bushfire smoke from Kuring-gai Chase, tallow-making smoke from Botany, and malt fumes from the breweries.

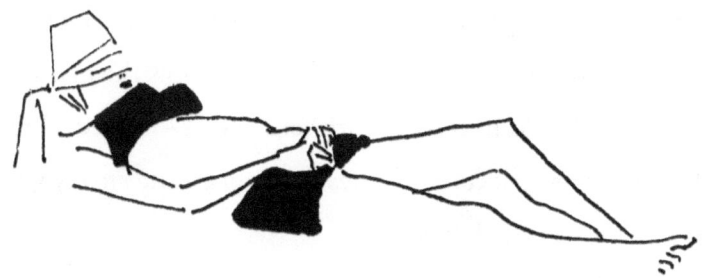

I mention this grimy mark on an otherwise spotless day because it was the only real evidence of a large city to be seen from Turimetta Head. The nearest suburb was Mona Vale. From there the houses spread south along the coast to Narrabeen, became more numerous at Collaroy, and then swerved out of sight up the hillsides of Manly and Balgowlah; but apart from that band of haze on the horizon, there was no way of telling how great or how small was the invisible city to which these visible suburbs belonged. The prospect consisted mainly of sea and bush.

To the north five dark headlands marched one behind the other into the haze; to the east nine racing yachts scudded down the coast, their spinnakers full of nor'-easter; and to the south a middling surf rolled towards the shore, breaking first against the Narrabeen cliffs, where its spume seemed to spread the rock platforms with lace, and farther south breaking in long white lines against the tan crescent of sand that runs from Narrabeen to Long Reef. Below the hissing of wind in a few banksias on Turimetta Head – indeed, almost below the level of consciousness – the deep and steady whisper of the sea was all around.

While the sea was thus asserting itself in sight and sound, the rising slope of bush behind Mona Vale was utterly passive. There was a bushfire somewhere that day, but the fire itself was out of sight, and the smoke in the air served only to drain the trees of what little colour they sometimes possess, and mercifully to obscure the Baha'i temple, which flaunts its Persian dome discordantly on the horizon. Vast and uniform, the bush made no claims on anyone.

The view from Turimetta Head is admittedly an oblique introduction to Sydney, subordinating the city, as it does, to bush and sea; but this is the very reason I have chosen it. The bush and the sea are essential to my view of Sydney, and I want to establish them securely.

The bush, or rather our conception of the bush, is still recovering from D. H. Lawrence's delineation of it in his novel *Kangaroo*. Lawrence never quite got used to seeing the constellation of Orion standing on its head with sword belt upside down, and this made him feel lonely and alien. He also shared the common misapprehension that because Australia had experienced no major crustal movements for aeons past, and consequently had a more even topography than, say, the Americas or Africa, it was geologically much older than the other continents. These fancied qualities determined the emotional response to the bush by Lawrence's central character, Richard Somers, from the moment he first strolled into it one evening in Western Australia:

> But the bush, the grey, charred bush. It scared him. As a poet, he felt himself entitled to all kinds of emotions and sensations which an ordinary man would have repudiated. Therefore he let himself feel all sorts of things about the bush. It was so phantom-like, so ghostly with its tall pale trees and many dead trees, like corpses, partly charred by bush fires: and then the foliage so dark, like grey-green iron. And then it was so deathly still. Even the few birds seemed to be swamped in silence. Waiting, waiting – the bush

seemed to be hoarily waiting. And he could not penetrate into its secret. He couldn't get at it.

Somers felt that Sydney was an intruder on its seemingly ancient landscape. 'It didn't seem to be real, it seemed to be sprinkled on the surface of a darkness into which it never penetrated.' He liked the harbour well enough, though:

> But the land, the ever-dark bush that was allowed to come to the shores of the harbour! It was strange that, with the finest of new air dimming to a lovely pale blue in the distance, and with the loveliest stretches of pale blue water, the tree-covered land should be so gloomy and lightless. It is the sun-refusing leaves of the gum trees that are like dark, hardened flakes of rubber.

I have quoted Lawrence at some length because these passages are nothing less than a catalogue of qualities that the bush does not possess. To start with, the bush is not gloomy and lightless. Somers was obviously looking in from outside. Had he walked into the bush by daylight he would have noticed, as Charles Darwin had done almost a century earlier, that it actually lets in far more light than a forest in the northern hemisphere. 'The trees nearly all belong to one family,' wrote Darwin in *The Voyage of the Beagle*, 'and mostly have their leaves placed in a vertical, instead of, as in Europe, in a nearly horizontal position: the foliage is scanty, and of a peculiar pale green tint, without any gloss. Hence the woods appear light and shadowless.'

Nor is the bush a silent place. Somers first saw it at night, and does not seem to have realised that the birds he fancied to have been so ominously quiet were merely fast asleep. I cannot say how many birds there are in the West Australian bush, but more than 370 different species have been sighted in Sydney over the years, and no one who has heard a flock of rainbow lorikeets squabbling and gorging on gum blossoms, or a gang of currawongs 'whistling like larrikins' on a wintry evening, would suggest that this population is ever swamped in silence.

Finally, the bush is not an ancient place. Certainly the sandstone highlands in the north and south of Sydney and the interjacent plains of shale were laid down some 180 million years ago, but most of the plant species in these regions have indulged freely in evolution. There are one or two exceptions: some of the tree ferns in Royal National Park are said to look much the same as their progenitors did 50 million years ago, and the palm-like burrawang belongs to a group of plants almost twice as old again. With this information to put him in the right mood, perhaps D. H. Lawrence could have extracted a sense of hoary waiting from the burrawang, but I have often looked at its prickly fronds on the hillsides around Bilgola, and they have never communicated any sense of antiquity to me.

So far I have been clearing the bush of certain false imputations. Now I must try to say what the bush is, as well as what it is not, and this will be more difficult. The bush is untidy, of course: dead leaves fall imperceptibly all year long, and so the ground is always covered with fresh litter. The bark sloughs off tree trunks like sunburnt skin (on angophoras this is a luminously beautiful process, but on some trees the dead bark hangs down in long shreds and only adds to the general disarray), there is no symmetry about the branches, and no logic in the great sandstone boulders that crop out bulbously between the trees.

The bush is also uniform, or rather it appears to be so. There are in fact several kinds of bush, each botanically distinct from the rest: the coastal heath, for example, where grass trees raise their spears in the stunted company of mallees, banksias and dwarf apples; the dry sandstone bush of Kuring-gai in the north and Woronora in the south, where banksias, scribble gums, blood woods and waist-high plants with spiny leaves have come to terms with a ground so porous that it holds water little longer than a sieve; and the wet bush, where blue gums, blackbutts, ironbarks and other stately eucalypts rise like temple columns from floors of kangaroo grass. The differences exist all right, yet what the mind persists in recalling are not these separate quantities but rather their highest common factor – an olive-green austerity.

Display is kept to a minimum, here by paucity of water, there by poverty of soil, and everywhere by equability of climate; the trees have no need to shed their leaves in winter, and thus no chance to burgeon in the spring. Consequently the appearance of the bush changes little throughout the year. In autumn the *Nephila* spiders build webs strong enough to snare blue wrens, and so thickly spun that in some gullies it is impossible to walk without carrying a stick to brush the webs aside; and in spring the sandstone bush colours up with pink boronia, red and white grevillea, white honey-scented heath, and yellow pea. But seasonal aberrations can no more upset the constancy of the bush than an acre or two of rainforest can spoil its uniformity. Spider webs last only a little while, and, with the single vivid exception of the waratah, the flowers of the bush are unobtrusive.

Indeed, the bush reminds me of one of its own lichen-covered boulders, hard, grey-green and apparently unchanging. I say 'apparently' because sandstone is by no means exempt from change. The wind frets it, Aborigines have chipped the outlines of men and beasts and birds on it, and white men have shaped it into building blocks. This also happens to the bush: the wind disturbs it, bringing rain and seeds and sparks, and humans put their marks upon it. The bush does change, but we are inclined to forget that this is so, for right up to the last moment – the moment of bushfire or bulldozer – it preserves an air of perfect stability.

Compare this now with the other half of the view from Turimetta Head. On the one hand there is the austere and passive bush, seemingly uniform in space and constant in time; on the other hand the active sea, variable in both space and time. The one keeps its distance and preserves its identity; the other intrudes, and changes by the mile and by the hour. On the day I am thinking of, the sea was bright blue, except for a strip of shallow aquamarine near the shore, but at other times it can be grey, green, and even red. At different times of the year a surface drift of tropical water tints the sea with square kilometres of green plant life or infinite millions of microscopic red organisms, and litters the shore with stranded blue-bottles and jelly fish. When a southerly wind collides with this drift, the sea rises up with its greatest force, smashes against the sandstone cliffs, moves sandbars, and makes and unmakes beaches from Barrenjoey down to Cronulla.

Halfway through the afternoon a shark patrol plane flew over Turimetta Head, casting a shadow on the grass and scaring the kestrel out of its equilibrium with the wind. No swimmer has been taken by a shark at any of Sydney's ocean beaches since 1936, when a fourteen-year-old boy disappeared in a flurry of bloodstained water at South Steyne, but so sudden and terrible are the attacks that have taken place inside the harbour that there can be few surfers who have not at some time or another imagined to themselves the fearful slash of unseen teeth on thigh and calf.

The first shark I ever saw was a grey nurse that had been caught off Curl Curl and put on display outside the surf club. I was only six or seven years old at the time, and was more interested in the contents of the shark's belly (four kittens, a felt hat, a seagull and several empty tins, all stacked neatly beneath the huge serrated jaws) than I was in the creature itself; but the fate of those drowned kittens was not lost upon me, and from that day onward I had a much better understanding of the word 'shark'.

Thus the shark patrol plane seemed to trail ripples of vague disquiet as it droned south through the afternoon looking for shadows in the aquamarine. Over Narrabeen and Collaroy it flew, over Dee Why, Curl Curl, Harbord, Queenscliff, North Steyne, and Manly; over the weird and lonely mesa of North Head, over the Gap at South Head, and over the pale yellow, almost white sands of Bondi, Tamarama, Bronte, Clovelly, Coogee and Maroubra.

Ben Buckler's sewer outfall, that great blotch on the sea which is called the Murk, had not spread far from the cliffs. This was something to be thankful for, but the wind that restrained the Murk also held back the surf, and the waves breaking at Bondi were nothing like those that sometimes afford the fastest board-rides in Sydney. 'You can get up to fifty kilometres an hour out there with a short board on a really big wave,' says the captain of Bondi Surf Bathers' Life Saving Club, a twenty-three-year-old baker named Warden Williams. 'You get a green wave, one that doesn't break. It'll stand right up. Then you cut it: you get on it and with a flick of your leg you're on an angle and you cut down the wave just like the big dipper at Luna Park'.

Bondi Beach is roughly sixty-eight metres wide, from surf to concrete promenade, and thus it manages to keep apart the two elements basic to all beaches – surf and sand, or exertion and ease. On a narrow beach such as Manly or Collaroy, with surfers coming and going all the while, exertion and ease are inseparably entwined; at Bondi the sunbathers near the promenade have scarcely any connection at all with the surf.

Down where the sand is wet, a crew is starting to drag the surfboat *Bird of Paradise* back to its shed. 'Okay, let's go!' yells the boat captain. 'Hey! Hey!' Drowsy heads rise from the sand, couples uncouple, and radios are lifted out of the way. Exertion has intruded upon ease, but not for long. Down go the heads again; back go the couples, the beach towels, the beach bags and the radios. In no time at all the furrow left in the sand by the surfboat's keel has been obliterated by the apparatus of sunbathing.

On a vastly greater scale than this minor intrusion, the sea itself intruded long ago upon the bush, flooding the deepest valleys with salt water and letting strange archaic fish glide silently through the trees. This is not a figure of speech, but geological fact. Port Jackson was once the valley of the Parramatta River, but half a million years ago, when the coming of the ice ages lowered the level of the sea by some sixty metres, the river began cutting deeply into its bed; then, as the ice-caps melted, the waters of the Pacific Ocean spilled inland up the main valley and up the valleys of what are now called Lane Cove River and Middle Harbour Creek. The bush at the bottom of these valleys was drowned, and then gradually buried in silt.

The waratahs and banksias soon disintegrated, but the harder bones of the bush are still lying there deep in the mud: during excavations for the Captain Cook dry dock, the stump of a bloodwood tree was found standing in the position of growth far below sea level.

Sydney Harbour, which may be taken to include all three drowned valleys and their various coves and bays, is like a hand reaching into the bush. 'It is shaped somewhat like an oak-leaf,' wrote Mark Twain, '– a roomy sheet of lovely blue water, with narrow offshoots of water running up into the country on both sides between long fingers of land, high wooden ridges with sides sloped like graves.' South of the harbour, the sea has also flooded the sunken plain now known as Botany Bay, and has pushed its way up George's River as far west as Liverpool. It has done the same on the northern side. From Turimetta Head one may see the shallows of Narrabeen Lagoon and the deeper, wider expanse of Pittwater between Barrenjoey Peninsula and the bush-covered ridges of Kuring-gai Chase. Beyond those ridges, lying deep in captured valleys, there is still more salt water: Broken Bay, Cowan Creek, Coal and Candle Creek, and Berowra Waters.

It is always rather surprising to come upon one of these arms of the sea in the middle of the bush. The track from St Ives down to Bobbin Head, for instance, comes at one stage to a sandstone shelf from which may be seen, far below and completely surrounded by hillsides of bush, a loch of olive-green water. The track drops steeply to Cowan Creek (for that is its name) and then follows the western bank downstream. A high wind moves noisily through the bush on the upper half of the eastern hillside, but there is no wind at water level. Sunshine slants down to the creek bed and lights up a school of mullet browsing at equilibrium against the incoming tide. The tide brings food from the sea, and perhaps it may also bring death; that dark shadow in midstream – could it be a shark?

It is hard to believe that sharks would come as far as this into the bush, yet they do, and the very improbability of their presence partly explains why so many fatal attacks have taken place in waters such as Cowan Creek. Bantry Bay, for example, seems so far from the sea that a young woman who waded in up to her waist there one afternoon in January 1942, probably gave no thought at all to sharks. A few minutes later she was bitten completely in two.

The shadow in midstream is not moving, and so it is probably a rock. But there are other less ambiguous reminders of the sea: the big white-breasted bird soaring overhead is a sea eagle, and the occasional mounds studded with oyster and cockle shells beside the track are kitchen middens built up over centuries by the Aborigines who once inhabited this valley, gathering their food from sea as well as bush.

Just as in that ancient time the world between Broken Bay and Botany Bay consisted only of sea and bush, the one eroding the other's cliffs, salting the other's fresh-water streams, sending its nor'-easters and southerlies to stir the other's treetops, and eventually bringing sails to the other's shores, so the city of today is a product of active and passive forces – the 'alien breezes' which Bernard O'Dowd mentioned in his marathon poem *The Bush*, and the native treetops that are stirred and changed by those breezes:

> Yet, there are moods and mornings when I hear,
> Above the music of the Bush's breath,
> The rush of alien breezes far and near
> Drowning her oracles to very death:
> Exotic battle-cries the silence mar,
> Seductive perfumes drive the gum-scent far…

Sydney began changing in earnest in the late 1940s, and since then I have lived here almost continuously. Thus I have been part of the change that has taken place during those years, and only by careful reconstruction – a taking-away of this which did not exist before, and a putting-back of that which did exist but has now vanished – can I recall the city as it was then. The war had just ended. Cigarettes were rationed, the city's only university was bursting with ex-servicemen, building materials were scarce, and the power supply was always likely to fail. Trams still clamoured through the streets with cabalistic destination symbols (a white disc on red for Bondi Junction, three green diamonds for Canterbury) and conductors working perilously on the running-boards, hotels closed amid climactic uproar at 6 pm, the city's tallest building (Australian Provincial Assurance, Martin Place) was only twelve stories high, and less than two per cent of the population was anything but Australian or British born.

This was the bush, so to speak, over which alien winds blew fitfully from the sea: the winds thrashed the big gum trees in wintertime, ruffled their blossoms in the spring, helped bushfires to blacken their trunks and scorch their leaves in the summertime, carried away their seeds in autumn, and brought clouds from the sea to water the new growth. The process was almost imperceptible, but its cumulative results are now plain to see. One day you look around you and realise that the bush has indeed changed; it is still familiar, but no longer the same.

2

I AM now going to set my theodolite on the arch of the Harbour Bridge, not only because the top of the arch overlooks every part of Sydney except the northern coastline we have already surveyed from Turimetta Head, but also because it affords a clear view of three very permanent marks in the trigonometry of the city – Botany Bay, Sydney Cove, and Parramatta. Don't flinch; this is not a history, and I shall have little enough to say about convicts, jailers, and emancipists. Yet every city must have a beginning, and before examining the new Sydney that has materialised during recent years I want to consider its dark and bloody genesis. But let there be no misunderstanding about my motives: I shall recall the distant past only out of propriety, and not with any intention of suggesting that it is more than marginally relevant to the present. In my view, the child of 1788 is no father to the man of today.

Ascending the arch of the Harbour Bridge is a rewarding experience; indeed, I would go so far as to say that it is well worth the fine for walking illegally up one of the two wide stairways that span Port Jackson like the rails of a giant rollercoaster. It is cheaper and safer to go legally, of course, and on my last visit to the top I was escorted by a maintenance man who talked a good deal about the fauna of the bridge.

'One day I saw a hawk on the edge eating a pigeon,' he said, as we began the long upward walk. 'I got out through the handrail, and did he get a fright! He grabbed the pigeon – he wasn't too frightened to forget that – and off he went. There was wheat and feathers everywhere on the arch. He'd torn the pigeon's crop open. Another day I found a dead rat on the upper chord. Looked like a kookaburra had dropped him; he was fairly battered. Sometimes you see budgerigars up here, too. Whenever the Zoo overbreeds, it releases a flock, and they always seem to make for the bridge. I've seen as many as thirty budgies sitting in a row up there near the flagpole.'

As we walked, the city steadily expanded until at last we could see it all: the jostling towers between Sydney Cove and Central Square, the dingy backyards of Woolloomooloo and Darlinghurst, the western suburbs sprawling almost to the Blue Mountains, the North Shore line running along the edge of Kuring-gai plateau, and directly below us the placid surface of Port Jackson, marked only by the wakes of ferries. 'You can see a lot of Sydney up here,' my companion remarked. 'I brought a photographer up once and he saw a locomotive getting up steam at Darling Harbour. "Where's that train going?" he asked me. "Let's watch it and see," I said. It followed the waterfront, went through that cutting at Pyrmont to the Blackwattle side, came out of the viaduct at the head of Iron Cove, and went back around through Leichhardt.'

At first the city seemed still and quiet, but soon I became aware of occasional twitches and murmurs down below. A gardener was mowing the lawn at Government House, and an arc-welding machine flickered at Kurnell. I could hear dockers chipping paint with hammers in Walsh Bay, and there was a faint pulse of cheering at a swimming carnival in the North Sydney Olympic Pool. With a little imagination I fancied I could also hear the grinding of poker machines at the Automobile Club, the staccato of electric typewriters in the AMP building, and even the crackle of muskets saluting the Union Jack on 26 January 1788.

This last sound was the faintest of all, for the echoes of Sydney's past are almost too faint for the modern ear. I have heard them on Ball's Head, where the shape of an Aborigine's hand, outlined on sandstone by a spray of masticated lime and food, survives almost in the shadow of the Harbour Bridge. I have also heard them in the sandstone gun rooms of Fort Denison, in some of the old houses at Parramatta and Windsor, and under the fig trees of Argyle Place. By and large, though, Sydney's past has been shouted down by its present.

Botany Bay, where Captain James Cook's *Endeavour* cast anchor in 1770, is now girded with oil refineries. There is a timeless enough quality about the rock at Kurnell on to which a cousin of Cook's wife, Midshipman Isaac Smith, first stepped ashore on 29 April, but only a few yards away the present tense blares out from a large public notice: 'A person shall not, in the said park (a) deposit or leave any litter, bottle, rubbish or refuse, except in a receptacle provided by the Trustees for that purpose (b) break glass, deposit or leave any offal, filth, dung, dead animal or any noisome, noxious or polluted substance (c) deface, damage or destroy any monument, tablet, authorised inscription, rock, timber, plant or equipment, fence, gate-post, wharf, jetty, building, road, path, picnic area, table, seat, sign or fixture.'

It was also in this bay that Captain Arthur Phillip reassembled his eleven ships at the end of their nine-months-long voyage from Portsmouth. Its shallow water and sandy soil were not to Phillip's liking, and after six days the fleet sailed around into Port Jackson, where it proceeded to disembark some thousand souls (including 755 male and female convicts) at the head of a cove with a freshwater stream. Phillip named this cove, and by subsequent extension the colony on its shores, in honour of the Secretary of the Home Office, Lord Sydney – not an imaginative choice, but preferable, I think, to Albion, the name which Phillip had first intended for the settlement. The stream, whose precious water was later stored in excavated sandstone tanks, predictably enough came to be called the Tank Stream.

It is hard to imagine the gully of the Tank Stream as it was in the last few years of the eighteenth century. The stream sprang from what is now Hyde Park, and flowed north between the present routes of George Street and Pitt Street to the harbour, which at high tide reached as far as the present site of Bridge Street. Gum trees grew there, and parrots flew like arrows overhead. George Street was at first called Sergeant-Major's Row, for Sydney was a garrison town as well as a penal settlement. Men walked the streets in irons, pulled ploughs like oxen, and nursed their hatreds. Violence was never far away. One day Drum-Major Benjamin Cook stopped a fight between a convict and a marine, and as he did so he heard another convict, George Eccleston, say, 'May all the bloody bougres be served so.' Fifty lashes for Eccleston.

Today the Tank Stream lies buried under stone and bitumen. It still flows from somewhere south of King Street to the harbour, which is now 180 metres from Bridge Street, but its bed is around five metres below street level and is paved with tiles. In fact, the Tank Stream is now a stormwater tunnel only one and a half metres high. I walked down it once with a Water Board inspector and had to crouch all the way, holding on to the stone and brick walls and sliding my gumboots along the greasy tiles. 'These tiles were brought out from Scotland,' said the inspector. 'They're very beautiful.' He cleared the slime away from one of them, and illuminated its pale yellow beauty with his torch.

Further along the tunnel he stopped to shine his torch on the wall. 'See that triangle chipped in the stone? That's a convict mark.' After forty minutes of sloshing and sliding we reached a wide chamber where the Tank Stream leaves its rubbish behind and spills over a weir into Sydney Cove. My companion examined the sludge behind the weir. 'I like to give visitors a souvenir before they leave,' he said. 'You find dozens of coins here.'

Gavin Souter

The gully of the Tank Stream may have vanished without a trace, but perhaps the agonies and hatreds of those early years left some imprints upon the city. Does the animus of George Eccleston survive in our own outlook to the extent that we still wish all the bloody bougres served so? I am tempted to maintain with the poet Robert D. FitzGerald that the past still frets our subconscious like a wind at the door. But does it really?

This brings me to the third permanent mark after Botany Bay and Sydney Cove – Parramatta. On 7 October 1800, a convict named Maurice Fitzgerald, one of the Irishmen who had taken part in an insurrection at Castle Hill, was tied to a tree near Parramatta and given 300 lashes by two floggers, Richard Rice and John Jonson. 'Rice was a left-handed man,' wrote an eye-witness of this punishment,' and Jonson was right-handed so they stood at each side and I never saw two trashers in a barn moove their stroakes more handeyer than those two man killers did…I was to leew'rd of the flogers and I protest, tho' I was two perches from them, the flesh and skin blew in my face as they shooke off the cats. Fitzegarrel Recaiv'd his 300 lashes. Doctor Mason (I never will forget him) use to go to feel his pulls and he smiled and sayd "this man will tire you before he will fail, – go on." It is against the law to flog a man past 50 lashes without a Doctor, and during the time he was geting his punishment he never gave as much as a word; only one that was saying, "Don't strike me on the Nick, flog me fair." When he was let loose two of the Constibles went and tuck hould of him by the arms to help him in the Cart. I was standing by he said to them, "let my arms go," struck both of them with his elbows in the pit of the somack and nock them boath down and then step in the Cart. I herd Doctor Mason say "that man had strength in nuff to two hundredd more."'

Robert D. FitzGerald is a descendant of that Dr Mason, and for him the wind still blows that blew his namesake's flesh from the cats-o'-nine-tails:

> That wind blows to your door down all these years.
> Have you not known it when some breath you drew
> tasted of blood?
> Your comfort is in arrears
> of just thanks to a savagery tamed in you
> only as subtler fears may serve in lieu
> of thong and noose – old savagery which has built
> your world and laws out of the lives it spilt.

If my roots were as deep in Sydney as FitzGerald's are ('Could I announce/that Maurice as my kin I say aloud/I'd take his irons as heraldry, and be proud'), I too might taste blood on the wind; but because I cannot taste it, and doubt whether many of my neighbours can either, I question the validity of some of the conclusions that are often drawn from the fact that Sydney began its life in chains.

Between 1788 and 1849, approximately 80,000 convicts were transported to New South Wales, which for part of that time included Port Phillip and Moreton Bay as well as the penal settlements at Sydney, Newcastle, and Port Macquarie. Unfortunately there is no way of telling how many emancipated convicts settled in Sydney, or of measuring the influence of their presence, heredity, and tradition upon the character of the city. This leaves plenty of room for speculation. At one extreme it is sometimes argued that Sydney still seems a violent and anti-authoritarian community, and that, *post hoc ergo propter hoc*, these characteristics derive from the days when Sydney was indubitably violent and resentful of authority. At the other extreme, it may be argued that the original trickle of convict blood has been so thoroughly overlaid by subsequent immigration – just as the Tank Stream has been overlaid by bitumen – that it exerts little or no influence upon the present. George Eccleston and Maurice Fitzgerald mean little enough to me. How much less do they mean to Joe Baiutti of Leichhardt?

Holding this second view myself, I maintain that the other interpretation not only confuses sequence with consequence but also exaggerates those qualities of the present which correspond to qualities of the past. We are not an exceptionally violent or insubordinate community, but knowing what we know about our own antecedents, some of us like to think we are so. Indeed, this form of self-deception might itself be regarded as a genuine imprint of the past. I would not argue with that.

Anyone wishing to depict Sydney as a violent city can easily find the right pigments, for a city of more than five million people provides plenty of scarlet and vermilion. From the top of the bridge I see the Ship Inn at Circular Quay, and recall two men I once saw fighting on the footpath there. They were puffing and hissing like snakes, and one of them was bleeding from the mouth. This is the only street fight I have ever seen in Sydney, and I remember it well both for that reason and because it reminded me of a small news item I had read in an old *Sydney Gazette*: 'Laft week a DESPERATE conflict took place between a Butcher and Blackfmith, the former of whom appeared more obftinate than wife; but from his ridiculous hardihood, at length obliged the Vulcan to decline further hoftility, from motives of compaffion.'

Down at the Quay I also see the City Morgue. I was there one night when an ambulance brought in a seventeen-year-old girl who had been killed in a collision on Spit Road. She was lying under a sheet, and the motorcycle constable who had attended the accident said she was a nice-looking girl, a blonde. They get all sorts of people at the morgue. 'Pretty Boy' Walker was taken there after someone had fired a machine-gun at him one evening from a moving car in Alison Road, Randwick, and so were the late drinkers who stumbled into the arms of the Mutilator in the dark lanes of Darlinghurst. The Mutilator was a monstrous prodigy who no more belonged to this city than a comet which flashes across the night sky. He was an English migrant of uncertain identity, and might just as well have sharpened his terrible knife in Liverpool, Boston, or Brisbane; he happened to be in Sydney, that was all. Yet such is our taste for notoriety that subconsciously we were proud to have him here. We invented jokes about the Mutilator, and found a place for him in our mythology.

From the top of the bridge I also see the wharves of Darling Harbour, and a violence of a different kind. 'What's the yike about?' the gatekeeper asks a gang of wharfies as they walk off a ship. 'Buggered if I know, mate!' replies one of the wharfies. 'We're just trying to find out. We know there's a blue on, but!' Perhaps the pano (foreman) has called for thirty bales in each sling, and the delegate on the job has decided that twenty-five are as many as the sling can safely carry. If the pano stands his ground and the wharfies are confident that a safety issue is involved, they may stop work until a Board of Review arrives to settle the matter; on the other hand, they may not wait for the Board. If someone walks off the ship, that usually tears it. The blue is on, and everyone walks off.

'We was down below on lead, stacking fifty-six-pound bars,' explains one wharfie. 'The boys had been battling for gloves, so I went up to the pano. I'd cut me fingers and that. The pano said, "See your delegate!" So the delo fronted him and said, "If we don't get gloves we'll walk off!" "No, y's are not getting gloves," he said, "and if y's bloody stop work y's are off the payroll!" So we walked off. The next thing they got a Board down on us. We got suspended for two days, but the next gang in that hold got gloves.'

Walking off is the supreme gesture of defiance and solidarity. It may be justified, as when gloves have been refused or sling loads are too heavy, but even when there is no excuse for it, and no prospect of industrial gain, this act of industrial violence provides certain emotional satisfactions for the wharfie: it is one in the eye for the boss ('May all the bloody bougres be served so!'), and it shows that the wharfie will stand by his mates. 'We're not under any obligation to anyone,' says Botsy Williams, who played football for Australia in 1911, and still holds a wharf labourer's medal at the age of seventy-six. 'You compare a wharfie with the collar brigade – why, he's a different man altogether. He isn't servile. He doesn't become part of it. They're like whipped dogs in other industries. I like working with men who'll back you up in a blue.'

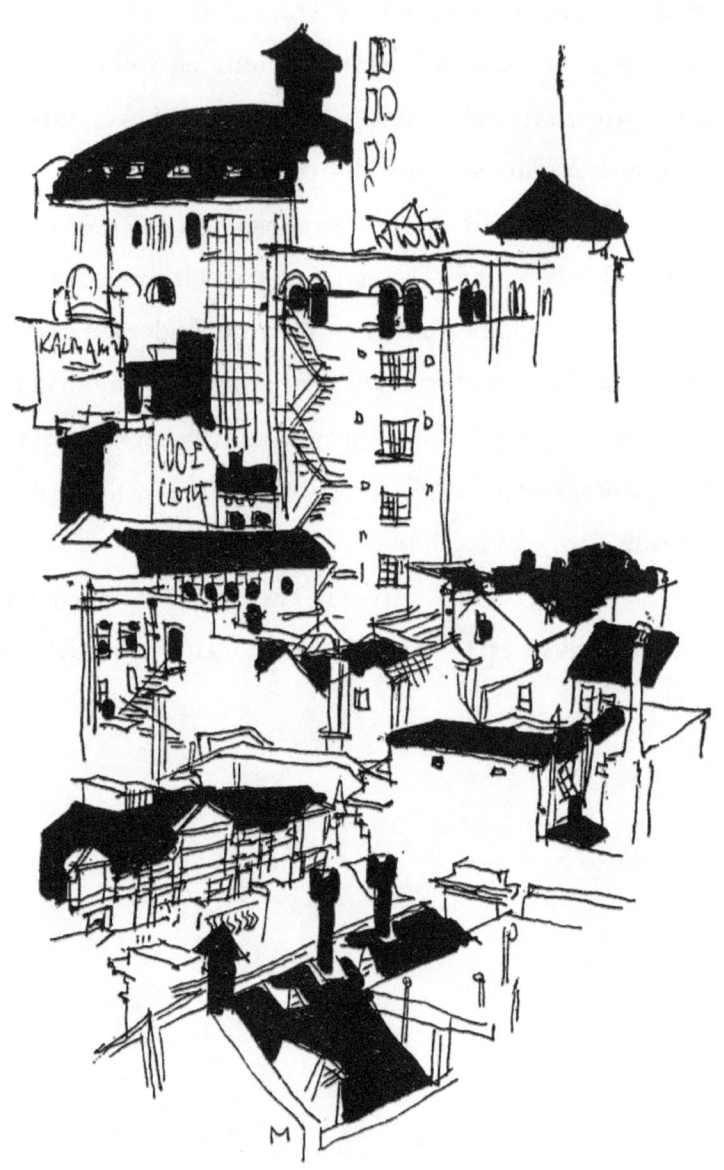

Although the waterfront conditions that once provoked such militancy have now disappeared, the militancy itself lingers on like a habit of which Botsy and his mates have no real desire to break themselves. Workers in most other industries are far less ready to walk off the job, not because they are whipped dogs but because conditions are generally good, yet even in the most affluent of these there lurks a predisposition to direct action which gains vicarious fulfilment from the wharfies' bloody-mindedness. The wharfie appeals to the striker in us all, and so he, too, finds a place in our mythology.

Another illusion we have about ourselves is that we resent authority, particularly as vested in the police force, and that we would all stand idly by while a mob of drunks put the boot into a helpless mug copper. This fits neatly into the convict interpretation of Sydney, yet honestly I cannot remember when a policeman was last assaulted with the connivance of a watching crowd. I have nothing against the police myself. Indeed, personal contact with them evokes from me a fawning goodwill, of which I later feel slightly ashamed, and I am sure that this is not an uncommon response. Legend insists that we are anti-authoritarian, and so it comes as something of a disappointment to realise that in fact most of us are quite docile. We are circumscribed by regulations ('Notice as to Penalties', 'Towaway Area', 'Notice as to Shopping Hours'), and when we are caught stepping out of line we usually go quietly.

There are some, however, who do not go quietly, who diverge magnificently from the norm, and these we celebrate because they help to preserve an illusion which otherwise we should lose entirely. I am thinking of George Fowler, who loudly proclaims that the earth is flat; of Arthur Stace, who goes around writing *Eternity* on the footpath; of Helena Winter, who spends most of her waking hours feeding stray cats; and particularly of Bea Miles, who never goes quietly, and who has not coincided with a norm since the days long ago when she attended Abbotsleigh Church of England School for Girls at Wahroonga.

The word 'Bea' has only one connotation in Sydney: it brings to mind a burly Rabelaisian woman with absolutely no sense of propriety; a woman so fascinated by public transport that she often rides all day in buses; a woman who plays patience in bank vestibules and court rooms; a woman who recites Shakespeare for a living, and who reveres the late Henry Louis Mencken. The three books which Bea values most, and which she often carries around in her satchel, are Mencken's *Chrestomathy*, Shakespeare's *Works* and *Gulliver's Travels*.

There is one passage in the *Chrestomathy* that fits Bea Miles like a glove. 'Perhaps one of the chief charms of women as figures in human society,' wrote Mencken, 'lies in the fact that they are relatively uncivilised. In the midst of all the puerile repressions and inhibitions that hedge them round, they continue to show a gipsy and outlaw spirit. No normal woman ever gives a hoot for law if law happens to stand in the way of her private interest.' This is indeed the essence of Bea's charm, and one cannot but be grateful to her for continuing to display that outlaw spirit which has been tamed in the rest of us, if in fact we ever did possess it.

The last time I saw Bea Miles in Central Court of Petty Sessions she was answering an offensive-behaviour charge – to wit, that she had forced her way into a taxi and refused to leave. This was the 203rd time she had been arrested. 'I told her I was not available for hire,' said the driver, 'and if she did not get out I would take her to Central Police Station. She refused. I can't recall the actual words. As I approached King Street she switched the ignition off and pulled the keys out of the lock, threw them on the floor, opened the door, got out, then pushed the door forward on to the front mudguard.'

Bea, attired as usually in an old floral frock, a pair of men's black shoes and a tennis eyeshade, was too busy scribbling on a piece of paper to pay much attention to this evidence. After the magistrate had wearily fined her £20, she passed a note to the press table. 'The police,' it read, 'have victimised me for 23 years for six reasons: (1) They can't make me leave the city (2) They can't get me on a criminal charge (3) Nor on a vice charge (4) Nor on a drunk ditto (5) They can't vag me (6) They can't get an honest doctor to declare me insane. I could not live in any other city than Sydney. Not only is it the most interesting city, it has the most temperate climate. Besides that, I have a great many privileges here; so the police may as well cease trying to put me out.'

Reading this manifesto now, I can almost believe that Sydney is a city of outlaws; listening to Botsy Williams, I can almost believe that it is a city of strikers; and remembering the Mutilator, I can almost believe that it is a city of prodigious murderers. I would like to believe all these things, for they could so conveniently be attributed to our history, but unfortunately I know that they are not really true. Apart from a certain readiness to believe the worst of ourselves, we are not indelibly marked by the past. The wind we know best is not the one that tastes of blood but the one I mentioned earlier – the one that blows in from the sea and disturbs the bush.

3

THE 'BUSH' I am thinking of now extends in space from Circular Quay to Central Station, and in time from as long ago as I can remember to some time during the last twenty years. The spatial boundaries are clear enough: on the east side, Farm Cove and Woolloomooloo Bay sway their seaweed against the sandstone rocks and walls of the Botanic Gardens; on the west, Darling Harbour carries its oily flotsam past the wharves of Sussex Street; and if these boundaries seem too wide, one can always settle for the City Circle which runs beneath Town Hall and Wynyard, bursts into sunlight and sparkle at Circular Quay, and then returns in darkness through St James and Museum to Central. Inside that circle lies the heart of Sydney.

The only trouble with this inner boundary is that it was not complete during the time I am trying to define; indeed, the rail link between Wynyard and St James is part of the wind that has disturbed the bush. As far as I am concerned, this bush dates back to the middle 1930s, when I first began to notice it. By that time the underground railway was running to Wynyard and St James, the Harbour Bridge had been built, Martin Place had been extended to Macquarie Street, and the inner city had acquired a few twelve-storey buildings. For the next twenty years it seemed as if this area would always be the same: Coogee and Maroubra trams would always climb noisily up Phillip Street, the jacaranda tree beside the Union Club would go on dropping its mauve flowers every summer, old Mr Tyrrell would preside over his bookshop near Wynyard until kingdom come, and the six o'clock swill at Aarons and Ushers would be repeated joyously forever.

Sometime in the 1950s – was it 1956, when the City Circle was completed? – the inner city gradually began to change, and by the 1960s it had changed almost out of recognition. The trams had gone, the jacaranda had been cut down and the Union Club demolished, Mr Tyrrell was dead and his bookshop had moved to a new address, the six o'clock swill had ended, and Aarons and Ushers were no more. In their place arose a new city: a city with buses instead of trams, and abstract sculpture instead of jacaranda trees, a city with a higher skyline and a wider outlook than before. Some time during the 1950s Sydney became more concerned about intellectual issues, less self-conscious about the arts, more permissive in its social attitudes, and less considerate of sacred cows. The literary gap between the little magazines and the daily newspapers was filled by *Nation* and the *Bulletin*; the

'Charm' school of painting was replaced by such non-figurative artists as John Olsen, Leonard Hessing, Stan Rapotec, and Carl Plate; the tentative non-conformity of the postwar bodgies and widgies expanded into the social freedom of the surfies, the beatniks, and the libertarians of the Royal George Hotel; theatre audiences that had once sat uneasily through Eliot and Fry somehow came to terms with Ionesco, Brecht, and Albee; and the satirical magazine *Oz* demanded and was granted a latitude that would have seemed incredible in the early 1950s.

The heart of this new city may be defined by the City Circle, but where shall I start to describe what lies within that circumference? I shall be guided in this by Alf Neilly, an old-age pensioner who prefers Circular Quay to all other parts of the city. I sometimes see him watching the ferries as they come to berth with a swirl of white foam and a creaking of rigid rope, or sitting on one of the seats outside the Customs House. The Cahill Expressway shuts out most of Sydney Cove these days, and the twenty-six floors of the AMP building keep some of the morning sun away; but there is salt in the air, and pigeons are continually landing and taking off from the little square in front of the Customs House. 'It's sheltered down here,' Alf told me once. 'The air is fresher than it is up the city, and you get a better type of person. Up Belmore Park, you get the metho fiends. I don't know how they can drink the stuff. I know what it tastes like: my old Dad used to be a French polisher, and when any of us kids got a toothache he'd give us a teaspoonful of metho to wash out the tooth with. It used to dry your mouth out, all right. Some of those up at Belmore Park buy a family size bottle at the grocer's for one-and-eleven and then mix it with water.'

The most remarkable thing about Belmore Park, near Central Station, is not its metho fiends but the cats that inhabit its trees. I have never seen them myself, for the plane-trees and trees of heaven in the park are high and thickly foliaged, but Mrs Helena Winter assures me that about ten cats live in the topmost branches during the day. At night they come down and eat the meat that Mrs Winter has left for them.

Every morning Mrs Winter chops up to fifteen kilograms of meat at her home in Rushcutters Bay, loads it into a shopping trolley and catches a bus up through Kings Cross and down William Street into the city. Sometimes she pulls her trolley through the Botanic Gardens, down past the white statues of Victorian children and Greek athletes, past the kiosk, the wishing tree, and the azaleas, to a colony of sleazy tabbies that inhabits a grove of palm trees near Mrs Macquarie's Chair. After leaving some meat there, she walks back to the city and catches a bus up George Street to keep other appointments. First she feeds Ginger and Mickey in a timberyard opposite Anthony Hordern's, next Mumma in Sussex Street, and then a gang of eleven sidling, purring, anonymous cats in the box yard behind the fish market. The boxes smell strongly of fish, but their smell is more tantalising than nourishing, and Mrs Winter's succour is more than welcome.

From the box yard she wheels her trolley down to the fruit and vegetable markets in a vain attempt to lure out a young tabby whom she is determined to have desexed. 'She has kittens after kittens after kittens,' says Mrs Winter. 'I've never been able to put a hand on her!' Over in the quiet shadows the tabby, hungry but intact, disappears silently behind a pile of banana crates.

Earlier in the day, five days a week, these markets are in a continual uproar while greengrocers and barrowmen belittle the finest produce they can see in the hope of breaking down its price. 'That's only a one-day apple, Norm!' says Charlie, a barrowman who operates in Bathurst Street. He is thick-set, and wears a cardigan, open-necked shirt, green felt hat and wide-cuffed flannel trousers. 'Nothing better than these, son? I'm looking for a good zacker.'

Norm produces a better apple. 'They got no colour,' says Charlie scornfully. He stops at a pile of navel oranges from Mildura and asks the price. Too high. 'I'm looking for a zacker,' he says moodily. 'What am I gunna use for a zack orange?'

The agent, a huge Chinese-Australian, appears genuinely shocked. 'I can't drop,' he says. 'Fingers are tied! I'd like to, Charlie, I'd like to. But fingers are tied. Ask Billy. He's your best chance.' Charlie takes another look at the navels. 'Mark us up three,' he mutters, and the agent chalks a big 'C' on three cases. Soon after 8 am Charlie drives his cases to Bathurst Street, where his partner has already set up the barrow. Lovingly he arranges the fruit in shiny tiers, and starts calling: 'Six for two bob the navels! Two for two bob the melons!'

The only other street cries in Bathurst Street are heard once a week from the Covenanters, an evangelistic group that meets here on Saturday nights. One of these evangelists is Arthur Stace, the little old man who wanders the city almost every day inscribing the word *Eternity* on the pavement with a bright yellow crayon. One night long ago Mr Stace, a reformed metho drinker and erstwhile cockatoo for a two-up school in Kippax Street, heard the evangelist John Ridley preaching from Isaiah 57:15 – 'For thus saith the high and lofty One that inhabiteth eternity, whose name is Holy.' 'Eternity! Eternity!' cried Ridley. 'Oh, that I could go out into the streets of Sydney, and say to every person, "Eternity! Where will you spend eternity?"'

From that moment on Mr Stace knew what he must do. He is in his eighties now, but still he rises almost every day at 4 am and goes out into the silent streets of the city. After wearing down a four-inch crayon, he catches a bus home to Pyrmont for breakfast. I have never actually seen him on the job, but I have seen his handiwork everywhere: outside the CIB, outside David Jones, under the brass plates in Macquarie Street, outside the philately shops in the Royal Arcade, on the ramp at Wynyard, on the steps of the GPO, and on the pedestrian island in Chifley Square.

Much as I admire Mr Stace's dedication, his copperplate message does seem rather out of place on the pavements of a city that is anything but eternal. *Eternity*, he declares in Chifley Square, yet looking around me I can hardly remember what this part of Sydney looked like a few years ago. Those poplars in the centre of the square used to stand beside the ivy-covered brick wall of a musty old building that housed Fred Jones' second-hand bookshop, a locksmith's business, Ye Olde Chelsea Tea Shoppe, and an antique shop with the names 'Tost and Rohu' over its front window. Tost and Rohu were taxidermists, but they had been gone from the building for many years. There used to be another old building near the poplars, but it, too, was torn down in the 1950s to make way for the extension of Elizabeth Street and the erection of the Qantas office block and hotel. From the pedestrian island in Chifley Square I see the ponderous Commonwealth Centre, the dark State Government tower a block away, and the big rectangular buildings of P. and O., Australian Guarantee Corporation and Pearl Assurance, and I try in vain to remember what was torn down to make way for them.

Eternity, declares Mr Stace at the corner of Pitt and Bridge Street, yet already I have forgotten the precise location of the grapevine that used to grow outside the Rhinecastle cellar, and the details of the intricate route that led between two offices and past a lavatory into the wide, high-roofed, roaring bar of Aaron's Hotel. I remember clearly enough the exquisite taste of the first middy at five o'clock, the urgent catching of Cathy's eye behind the bar, and then the quenching of conversation and the rude gathering-up of empty glasses at three minutes to six. But all this belongs to the past. Aaron's and half a dozen other city hotels have crumbled under the hammers of Whelan the Wrecker; the extension of trading hours has taken much of the urgency out of drinking; and even the best of the old city hotels have changed their appearance to meet competition from new hotels and poker-machine clubs. Adams Hotel still rejoices in its vulgar marble columns and lovely Julian Ashton nudes, but its days are surely numbered.

Eternity, declares Mr Stace outside the old *Sydney Morning Herald* building, yet the pavement in Hunter Street no longer vibrates at night with the roar of underground presses, as once I thought it always would. Although the AMP building has been replaced by part of Australia Square, and the old Stock Exchange by Commercial Union House, it is the absence of the *Herald* that is most noticeable here. If the *Herald* building had been demolished it could easily be forgotten, but the triangular building still stands on the peninsula between Pitt, Hunter, and O'Connell Streets – a constant reminder of old times. The reporters' room where I used to work is now occupied by chartered accountants, and the composing room is an office of the Southern Pacific Insurance Company. Something the same has happened in Elizabeth Street: on the tiled wall of the Government Insurance Office is a ceramic representation of the charioteer who drives his seven horses out of the sunrise on the masthead of *The Sun*, and even there amid the third-party and workers' compensation claims this symbol still has the power to call forth memories of Sunday mornings with Ginger Meggs, Speed Gordon, and Cousin Marie.

Both the *Herald* and the *Sun* are now published elsewhere. For those who took part in it, this move outside the inner city has had the rather curious effect of seeming to increase the rate at which the inner city has been changing. The *Herald* left Hunter Street just as the building boom was starting, and ever since then I have been observing its progress not as a local inhabitant to whom the process of change has been so familiar as to be almost imperceptible, but rather as a visitor whose periodic glimpses of different parts of the city have added up to a sort of time-lapse photography. Buildings have disappeared overnight, and the city has opened new petals of aluminium and glass like one of those time-lapse flowers that take only a few seconds to bloom.

Just as the inner city once seemed unlikely ever to change, now it seems unlikely ever to stand still again. The other day I counted sixteen cranes on the skyline. The upper air rings continually with the erection of girders, and somewhere a dogman is always rising overhead. It is too early yet for a final verdict on the new city, but already I prefer it to the old. I like the altitude of its buildings (the revolving restaurant on top of Australia Square tower is 167 metres above sea level), and I like the way many of the buildings cover only part of the allotments on which they have been erected. There is admittedly a sameness about the new glass boxes, an international homogeneity that fits as glibly into Sydney as it would into San Francisco or Buenos Aires, but this orthodoxy is partly offset by the massive nonconformity of the Opera House on Bennelong Point, and in any case I much prefer the light and efficiency of the glass boxes to the sombre fussiness of the Edwardian and Victorian ages.

This is not to say that I would wish to see the city lose all its brown sandstone piles. I hope that the Lands Department building with its twenty-one external statues (Sir Henry Parkes, W. C. Wentworth, John McDouall Stuart, *et alii*, all holding documents of State, or shielding their sandstone eyes against the inland sun) is never pulled down, and that Sydney's aldermen never tire of the superlatively ugly Town Hall, which was designed over a period of twenty years by no fewer than five different architects. I like the GPO, the clock tower at Central Station, the Customs House at Circular Quay, St James' Church and most of the other buildings designed by Francis Greenway, but otherwise I am perfectly willing to surrender everything built before 1930. Let Whelan the Wrecker do his worst.

Eternity, declares Mr Stace in Martin Place, yet even here there are traces of change. Martin Place was the centre of the building boom in the 1930s, and since then its physical appearance has changed little more than the Moruya granite of the Cenotaph. The GPO clock tower was taken down as an air-raid precaution during World War II, and its eventual restoration was a figurative as well as a literal instance of putting back the clock: when the five-ton bell chimed once more for Anzac Day the lower half of Martin Place looked and sounded exactly as it had a quarter of a century before.

But appearances can be deceptive. Martin Place is the hallowed ground upon which we pay homage, and payments of that kind are not as constant as granite; they are subject to change. Let me illustrate this by describing three days of homage in late autumn: Anzac Day (25 April), Empire Day (24 May) and Coral Sea Day (7 May).

Anzac Day begins at dawn, when two columns of men come marching down Martin Place. There is no tramping of boots, only a whisper of shoe leather as the columns draw level with the Cenotaph, and an uneven patter and jingle of medals as they halt and turn. 'At this hour upon this day, Anzac received its baptism of fire and became one of the immortal names in history. We who are gathered here think of the comrades who went out with us to the battlefields of the Great War, but did not return. We feel them still near us in the spirit...' As the words of the Anzac dedication die away, a bugler sends the hard, sad silver of the Last Post flowing out into the dark, and an old man on crutches starts to cry.

It was a hot day this year, and by evening Martin Place was looking rather worn. The steps of the GPO were littered with newspapers and crusts left by those who had sat there to watch the march, there were some beer bottles in the gutter, and the flowers on the Cenotaph were already starting to wilt. A small crowd was still standing around the Cenotaph, reading the cards on the wreaths: 'In loving memory of my son Corporal D. Kidd, killed in action at El Alamein. Always remembered, Mum'... 'Pte Thomson S. F. 2/2 Machine Gun Battalion. In loving memory of our dear son and brother who was killed at Buna, New Guinea, 4th September, 1943 – Mum, Shirley and Keith'... 'In memory of Ray Taylor 2/19th Batt. 8th Division. Killed in Malaya. Remembered by his wife Bess and twin sons Ray and Charlie...'

The spirit of Anzac is still strong, but no longer sacrosanct. 'Best we forget', advises *Oz*, and during Sydney University's Commemoration Week, which also falls in late autumn, someone hangs a clothesline full of scanties between the bayonets of the soldier and the sailor on the Cenotaph. This would never have happened in the 1930s.

Our second day of homage is Empire Day. On this day the Eastern Command bandsmen still march down Martin Place decked out in white pith helmets and imperial scarlet, but what are they celebrating? The Queen's birthday, the grandeur of Empire, or perhaps a sense of fellowship with the 'old country'? None of these things, really: 24 May is Queen Victoria's birthday, not Queen Elizabeth's; the Empire has ceased to exist, and the day itself is now officially known as Commonwealth Day; and as for fellowship, there has been a marked weakening of our emotional links with Britain in recent years.

'Sydney is more exclusively English in its population than either Liverpool or London,' observed a visitor in 1846. 'Were it not for an occasional orange tree in full bloom, or a flock of little green parrots whistling as they alight for a moment on a housetop, one might fancy himself at Brighton or Plymouth.' This was never really true, for we have always been Irish and Scottish as well as English, and for the last two decades we have been growing steadily less British. In 1947 only two per cent of Sydney's population had been born outside Australia or the United Kingdom; in the 1960s it was ten per cent. Today it is almost thirty per cent.

The other principal reason for a decline in our sense of Britishness is the knowledge that Britain can no longer protect Australia: only America saved us from Asia last time, and only America could save us again. So we are left with nothing to celebrate on Empire Day, unless it be our flimsy relationship with Ghana, Malawi, and the rest. The truth is that Empire Day has degenerated into Cracker Night, a night on which we explode fireworks for no reason at all.

On the third day of homage, Coral Sea Day, there are always two or three American warships in port to blow the coals of our gratitude. A US Marine Corps band from Honolulu and a Royal Australian Navy band march down Martin Place playing Sousa, a khaki and gold Admiral of the Seventh Fleet lays a wreath on the Cenotaph, and a flight of carrier bombers swishes overhead. This may not be our most enjoyable act of homage, but there is no questioning its validity. At Gallipoli we came of age; in the Coral Sea we had our national life saved.

There is another autumn day – in fact the last day of autumn, 31 May – which we do not celebrate. It is the day, or rather the night, on which four Japanese submarines invaded Sydney Harbour. I shall have more to say about this later; in the meantime I would like to mention one more change that has taken place in Sydney. Not only have we become slightly less reverent about Anzac Day, and exchanged our faith in Britain for dependence on America; we have also become aware of Asia.

Sydney has long had a Chinese community, and before the war we had a few Japanese woolbuyers. The Chinese are still here, endowing the southern part of the inner city with its only real character; the Japanese wool buyers are back in greater force than ever, buying more of our wool than even Britain does; car salesrooms in William Street offer Toyotas and Datsuns as well as Holdens and Falcons; our universities have enrolled thousands of Chinese, Malayans, Indonesians, Thais, Burmese, and Indians; some of our secondary schools now teach Bahasa Indonesia; and the city has one Malayan restaurant, one Indian, one Indonesian, three Japanese, and

132 Chinese restaurants. When I said earlier that the lower half of Martin Place had not changed for the last quarter of a century I was forgetting something. There is now a sukiyaki room between Pitt and Castlereagh Streets, just up from the Cenotaph.

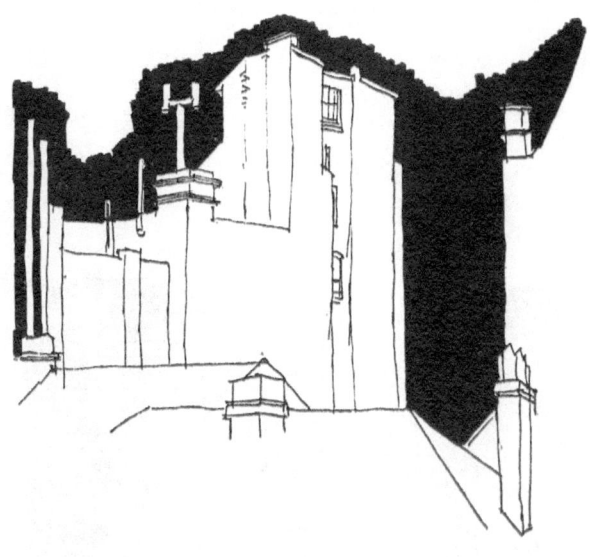

4

IN CROWN STREET there is a terrace house, old and unkempt, which seems to embody an essence of all the terraces around the inner city – a distillation of leaking gas, frangipani scent, wet mould, and budgerigar chatter. I suppose there are hundreds of others just like it, but surely none more representative. It has a fence of cast-iron spears across its three-metre frontage and a veil of cast-iron lace along the upper verandah; its stucco walls have needed a coat of paint for at least twenty years, some of the slates are missing from its roof, and the lace is rusting. Indeed the only pleasing thing about this façade, apart from a certain sturdiness of design, is the flowering frangipani in the tiny front garden.

The present owner, Mrs Tomlinson, has lived on the top floor since the death of her husband thirty-two years ago. She lets the ground floor, and has not always been fortunate in her choice of tenants: the last tenant seemed respectable enough, but one evening someone fired a bullet at him through the front window, and he moved out the next morning. The bullet made a neat hole about the size of a shirt button. There was no untidy shattering, so Mrs Tomlinson did not bother to have the pane replaced.

The top floor is rather cramped for space, but Mrs Tomlinson has all she needs: a gas ring and shower recess at the back, a wedding photograph and a portrait of her late husband on the bedroom wall, and beside her bed a radio surmounted by a flamingo made of shells, its pink base embossed with the words, *Love Faileth Never*.

Underwear and a pair of white gloves are drying on a line slung across one of the front windows, and at the other window there are two cages – a small peach-face parrot in one, a lovebird in the other.

'Another little budgie flew in last week,' she told me once, 'and landed on Peter's [the parrot's] cage. Peter gave him what-for, nearly bit his leg off, but I caught him in time and borrowed a cage for him. Then this lady from down the street came in and said the butcher had told her that I'd found a lost budgie. She was all trembling, she was that excited. It was him all right. Do you know what she called him? I'd been calling him all the names I could think of, and he didn't perk up at any of them. She called him Muscles.'

So homogeneous is the terrace world that almost every home has its own budgerigar – a chirpy daub of emerald, lapis lazuli or gold on an otherwise sombre background. The other day I saw a green one among some sparrows on the lawn at Crown Street Women's Hospital. It might have been Muscles on the loose again.

During the 1880s and 1890s terrace houses like Mrs Tomlinson's were built by the thousand to accommodate the city's expanding force of industrial labour. From Pyrmont in the west their herringbone rooftops spread through Redfern and out to the northern slopes of Paddington, up over Surry Hills and down through Darlinghurst to Woolloomooloo. The tenants were poor. Many of them were law-abiding people living as best they could; many were larrikins, stand-over men, harlots, and no-hopers.

At different but overlapping periods the Plunkett Street Push and the razor gangs roamed the streets and lanes of Woolloomooloo, the late Kate Leigh presided over her sly-grog domain at Surry Hills, Kicker Kelly and Jazzer O'Connor jointly ruled the two-up roost in Darlinghurst, and Chicka Barnes pursued his violent trade as a stand-over man. It was at the Kelly-O'Connor school one night in 1944 that the young Chicka Barnes ran into his first real blue. Chicka had a way of pretending that he had won the toss, scooping up the pool, and then, when the other players protested, returning most of it to the floor; a fiver or two undoubtedly stayed in his pocket, but up till then nobody had ever called his bluff. On this occasion he left the school rather hurriedly, and was later found lying in Bourke Street with four bullet wounds in the stomach. Chicka was only twenty-four then, and he survived to live another thirteen years before his life was ended by a single bullet in the back. At the inquest into his death the surgeon who removed the fatal bullet recorded all the traces of old wounds on Chicka's body. It was a terrible list: four bullet scars on the lower abdomen, one finger shot from the left hand, two stabbing scars on the chest, a scar where someone had once tried to cut his throat with a butcher's knife, the scars left on his forehead and shoulders when two men thrashed him with a mattock and bicycle chain, and numerous smaller scars on the chin and lips, trademarks of street fighting.

For reasons I shall come to later, the old terrace world between the city and the suburbs has quietened down a lot since the days of Kate Leigh, Kicker Kelly, and Chicka Barnes; but certain parts of Darlinghurst are still stubbornly unregenerate. People have been murdered there in broad daylight, and the brothels of Chapel Street and Woods Lane are usually open for business both day and night. 'Come on, love!' calls a hefty lady in one of the lighted doorways. 'What are y's all standing there for like a lot of wet prawns?'

If Darlinghurst is the bullet hole in the window of the terrace world, then Kings Cross is the lovebird in its lounge room. Kings Cross is not a suburb, not a ward, not even a postal address, yet it has more identity than perhaps any other part of Sydney. 'Topo william street' it used to be called, and indeed its front door is still a gaudy jumble of illuminated signs ('The Pink Pussy Cat', 'Hasty Tasty', 'Stripperama') at the top of Sydney's stateliest thoroughfare. In 1897 the City Council bestowed the name Queen's Cross on the junction of William Street, Darlinghurst Road, Victoria Street and Bayswater Road, and eight years later it removed any confusion with Queen's Square by changing the Cross's sex. Sex has always been somewhat equivocal at the Cross.

From this junction at the top of William Street, Kings Cross has projected its identity up Victoria Street as far as the Slamat Makan Indonesian restaurant, and down as far as the Swiss Inn; up Darlinghurst Road as far as the Tabou near Elizabeth Bay Road; down Macleay Street to the Chevron-Hilton; down Bayswater Road to the All Nations Club; and down William Street to Brougham Street, where Rosaleen Norton used to burn her incense to Pan and Hecate. Perhaps she still does. It is a few years now since I visited Miss Norton's terrace house, but I recall the occasion clearly. It was about 11 am, and although bright sunlight was slanting through the leaves of the plane-trees downstairs, the Norton living room was kept dark with heavy drapes. Against one wall stood an altar decorated with a painting of Pan and a set of stag's antlers. The name *Uriel* had been chalked in several places on the wall. 'I must take those off,' said Miss Norton apologetically. 'They were put up for a particular operation – an invocation.'

Before I left, Miss Norton jokingly put on a rubber lizard's head mask. 'A friend of mine wore this to the Kashmir one night,' she said. 'It had all the tapuls quite worried.' A tapul, in case you are not familiar with the word, is a dummy made for occult purposes by a Tibetan sorcerer; in the occult coterie at Kings Cross the word is used to describe the 'non-us'. Miss Norton, her eyebrows pencilled upwards in Mephistophelean curves and a talisman around her neck, may sometimes be observed sitting among the tapuls at the Kashmir coffee lounge – an object of timid curiosity, like a lovebird among sparrows.

Kings Cross has forty-two coffee lounges like the Kashmir, twenty-seven restaurants, sixteen frock shops, eleven fruit shops, nine nightclubs and strip shows, and eight florists. This is the industry that caters for the thousands of visitors who swarm into the Cross each night; it sings to these innocents, strips for them, feeds them, shocks them, solicits them, laces their coffee with vodka, takes their money, and sends them home to Chatswood or Kingsgrove feeling that they have done something exciting, perhaps even faintly illicit. I may be an innocent from the suburbs myself, but I am convinced that Kings Cross is more than the sum of these commercial parts: at the Cross I will swear there is more emotional electricity in the air, the women are more handsome (if they are women, that is), nerve-ends are more exposed, and other people's conversations are louder and more interesting than anywhere else in Sydney. For example, two blondes who might be usherettes relaxing after an evening session are talking over coffee at the Piccolo Espresso, '…and he as good as said if I saw Bobbie again he'd kill me. It was a terrible thing to say…'

But I have wandered away from the point. The lovebird in the lounge room and the bullet hole in the window are not the whole terrace house, and to present the house as a whole I must now describe three newcomers to the terrace world, and try to show how they are changing it. Someone has painted *No Dagos* on the footpath in Crown Street, and this is probably an accurate enough expression of the old inhabitants' attitude towards the Italians, Greeks, and Maltese who have invaded Surry Hills, Darlinghurst, and Woolloomooloo since the war. 'The foreigners next door to me,' says one old girl in Riley Street, 'buy a rooster at the markets, tie its feet together, cut its throat in the bathroom, and hang it up dripping into the bath. That's the sort of people they are. Wherever you see a house that's just been painted, you can bet it's been bought by a foreigner.'

There is something not quite proper, she implies, about painting houses. Looking down Riley Street, you can certainly pick the newcomers by their mauves, pinks, greens, and whites, and by the *Valetta* and *Korinthos* nameplates that have replaced *Kia Ora* and *Emoh Ruo*. Carlo Mesiti has also replaced his frangipani with a stand of sugarcane to remind him of his cane-cutting days in North Queensland. Five years ago Mr Mesiti bought a terrace of four houses, painted them, knocked down their backyard fences, and planted a vineyard. 'It no matter where you live,' he says, 'you can make it decent. Meself and me family, we work like a slave to make this place like she is.'

The 'foreigners' are hard-working people with strong family discipline, and they give the Welfare Department and the police very little trouble. 'They are nearly all from Calabria down here,' says the priest who celebrates Italian mass at St Columbkille's in McElhone Street. 'They are like a clan, like a family.' Clannishness produces secure, law-abiding families, but it also retards assimilation. The Labour League in Woolloomooloo has no Italian members at all.

The same sort of thing happens elsewhere – among the Italians at Leichhardt, the Germans at Bankstown, the Yugoslavs at Mona Vale. In the 1940s there were only 36,000 people of foreign, non-British birth in Sydney; in the 1960s there were a quarter of a million; today the number is well over one million. A change of such magnitude and speed as this has naturally affected the city's character: collectively we are now a little less parochial and perhaps a little more conservative; we eat more adventurously, and drink more wine; and we have become more interested in soccer. These are the approximate limits of integration between Latins, Teutons, and Slavs on the one hand and native Celts and Saxons on the other. There is no serious friction between the two groups; just a lack of natural colloquy. The talking starts in the second generation.

A second type of newcomer to the terrace world is not really new at all. Aboriginal families have always lived here, but in the 1960s they were reinforced by new arrivals – one might almost say refugees – from the country towns of New South Wales.

In 1788 Governor Phillip estimated the number of Aborigines living between Broken Bay and Botany Bay at 1500. They were hunters and fishermen, and by most accounts were a gentle people. Dr George Worgan called them an 'active, volatile, unoffending, happy, merry, funny, laughing, good-natured, nasty, dirty race,' and Captain Watkin Tench, describing the reaction of several Aborigines to the flogging of a convict who had stolen some fishing-tackle from a native woman, concluded that they were 'not of a sanguinary and implacable temper'. 'There was not one of them,' wrote Tench, 'that did not testify strong abhorrence of the punishment, and equal sympathy with the sufferer. The women were particularly affected; Daringa [the owner of the fishing-tackle] shed tears; and Barangaroo, kindling into anger, snatched a stick, and menaced the executioner.'

Smallpox, rum, and miscegenation soon put an end to these inoffensive people. The last local full-blood died in 1857, and although it is probable that some of the Aborigines now living in the city are descended from Daringa and her sisters, the great majority of the population is undoubtedly migrants.

Every week or so a few more arrive from Coraki, Moree, Coonabarabran, or Nowra looking for the employment and dignity that are so scarce in the country. Some of them are lucky; others achieve only a change of address. There are people of Aboriginal descent in at least seventy different suburbs, but only at La Perouse, Blacktown, and Redfern are their numbers large enough to be noticed. They like living next to one another, and landlords take advantage of this by raising the rent.

Mrs Rita Davis was fifteen when she came to Sydney. Her parents had separated many years before, and she had spent most of her childhood with an uncle and aunt at Kyogle. 'They had a lovely house,' she recalls. 'It had eight rooms, with high rafters, and there was wisteria around the verandah. Us kids used to ramble all over the place. I remember one day I found a passionfruit vine growing in an old piece of cow manure if you please, and I brought it home and planted it beside the fence and it grew for years. On summer evenings we used to sit outside and eat melons. I had a wonderful childhood.'

Down in Sydney, Rita stayed with her father at Redfern, and became a machinist at a clothing factory. At the age of seventeen she married an Aboriginal sawmill worker who took her to live at Moree. After nine years, by which time Rita had eight children and was three months pregnant with the ninth, the husband deserted her. She battled on in a shanty house outside the town until her baby was born, then took the children to Redfern, where she was lucky enough to rent a terrace house for £8 a week in Louis Street. Somehow they all manage to survive on the Social Service pension, and on food and clothing parcels from a city charity.

The third type of newcomer to the terrace world is also a fugitive – not from Europe or the country towns, but from suburbia and all the restrictions and pretensions he imagines that word to imply. Not for him the red-brick bungalow and septic tank, the forty-minute train ride to work, unmade footpaths, and Progress Association meetings; instead he buys an old terrace in Paddington or Balmain, just a few minutes from the city, puts on a new roof, replaces the floorboards, rips out a wall or two, paints the remaining walls white, hangs up his Sepik wood carving and his guitar and his Ian Fairweather, and paints the exterior colony blue or slate grey, with lace all picked out in white. Out the back he plants a herb garden, a lemon tree, and a clump of miniature bamboo.

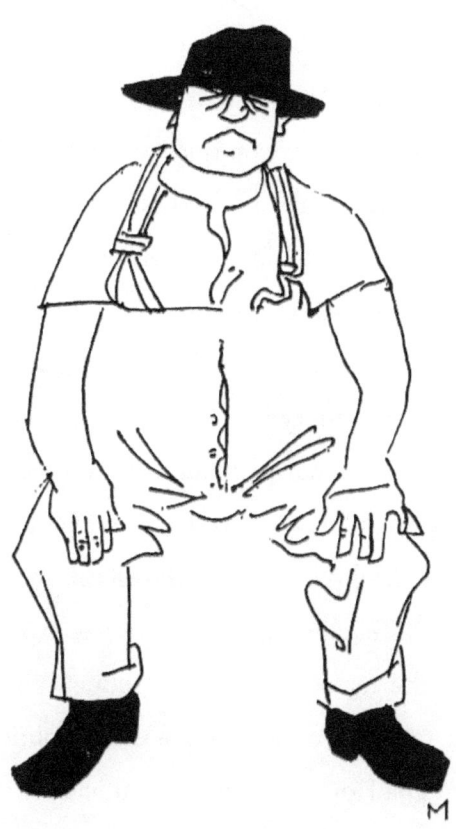

This rejection of suburbia carries great satisfaction for the renovator – who may be an architect, an artist, a poet, an actor, or an advertising executive – and for the terrace world it carries a new lease of life. Paddington Road and Jersey Road look better now than they have ever looked before. Nothing could better illustrate the change that has come over Paddington than a building at the corner of these two renascent streets – the Rudy Komon art gallery. Mr Komon stands in the same relation to Sydney's art market as Alastair Urquhart or Lionel McFadyen does to the Stock Exchange; he is one of its biggest brokers, and his art shows open with just as large a crowd, just as many sherries, just as much talk, and just as little interest in the works on display as do those at any of the nine other fashionable galleries in Sydney. On such occasions the gallery is packed with artists, wide-eyed aficionados, narrow-eyed speculators, art critics, newspaper columnists, social reporters, beautiful women, bored husbands, and beautiful young men. And all this in Paddington!

While the foreigners and the fugitives from suburbia are restoring the terraces, the City Council and the State Government take the easier course of demolition and reconstruction. The Housing Commission has demolished six acres of some of the most squalid housing in Surry Hills, and in its place has built Sir John Northcott Place, a vast brick citadel containing 643 flats. Sydney is undoubtedly better off without streets like O'Sullivan and Pearl, which have now disappeared forever, but some of the people who lived in those streets were sorry to leave them. They were given the choice of waiting for flats at Sir John Northcott Place or taking a Housing Commission home in one of the western suburbs. Only five families waited for flats; the rest of the little world in O'Sullivan and Pearl Streets was swept out to Villawood and Lalor Park.

Billy Jarvis, born in O'Sullivan Street some forty years ago, is a case in point. He lives at Lalor Park now, but every chance he gets he is back in the bar at the Forresters, on the corner of Riley and Foveaux. 'I know everyone round here,' he explains. 'But it's not like it was. I had some good mates and that in O'Sullivan Street. Real good mates. One of me best mates went to Brighton-Le-Sands, and another one went to Villawood. You understand what I mean?'

5

'BEFORE us lay the trackless immeasurable desert, in awful silence. At length, after consultation, we determined to steer west and by north, by compass, the make of the land in that quarter indicating the existence of a river. We continued to march all day through a country untrodden before by a European foot. Save that a melancholy crow now and then flew croaking overhead, or a kangaroo was seen to bound at a distance, the picture of solitude was complete and undisturbed.'

Thus in 1789 Captain Watkin Tench made his way through some of the far western suburbs – Wentworthville, Toongabbie, Girraween, Seven Hills, and Blacktown. The inland suburbs are now anything but quiet and lonely (indeed they accommodate rather more than half the population of Sydney), yet in some respects Tench's description is still valid. This part of the city may not be a desert, but it *is* flat and dry and largely devoid of vegetation.

The inland suburbs are by no means trackless, either, but they *are* shapeless, and a region with neither shape nor design can be just as bewildering as one without tracks. Parramatta Road, the Hume Highway, Canterbury Road, and Prince's Highway are all intersected by a dozen major lateral roads; five interconnecting railway lines run south-west, due west, and north-west from Central Station; and the whole intricate network is unrelieved by any landscape variation. There are no plateaux or ridges, no rivers to speak of, and no intruding arms of the sea. All one can say geographically about this amorphous suburban mass is that it lies between Port Jackson and the Parramatta River in the north and Botany Bay and George's River in the south, that it starts somewhere along the western margins of the inner city and the eastern suburbs, and that it runs westward for some fifty kilometres before petering out in farmland and virgin bush. It is not immeasurable, as Tench's desert seemed to be, but until its allotments become larger beyond Liverpool and Parramatta one might think that the tide of brick, fibro, and bitumen was never going to end. Sydney in fact covers more space than almost any other city in the world.

No one knows it all. You may know the Illawarra line painfully by heart – the railway workshops at Redfern, the brickpits at St Peters, and the uniform suburbs of Rockdale,

Kogarah, and Carlton. But who on this line knows where Yagoona is? Or Panania, Carramar, Narwee? These are stars in different galaxies, and it is not easy to think of them as a whole.

One day I watched a tree being cut down at Villawood. It was just about the last tree in sight, a handsome black-butt measuring two metres around the bole, and I should have thought that the local people would have gone to almost any lengths to preserve it; but no, one of its branches had fallen in a high wind, so down it had to come. As it lay by the side of the road, I noticed a split which apparently ran right up the middle of the trunk. This was a wind-shake, the tree-feller told me, a weakness produced in some trees by prevailing westerly winds: the windward side of the trunk is so often in a state of tension, or stretching, and the leeward side in a corresponding state of compression, or squeezing, that eventually the trunk splits inside.

I am reminded of this now by the inland suburbs. Out there a kind of windshake runs invisibly from Hurstville through Belmore to Strathfield. On its leeward side, back through Burwood, Ashfield, Leichhardt, and Dulwich Hill, the great suburban trunk has been compressed by almost a century of development. This side was built out long ago, and in areas where factories have replaced houses it has lost population. On the windward side, out through Bankstown, Liverpool, Fairfield, and Blacktown, the reverse is happening: suburbia is stretching its legs, and population is increasing at a rate Sydney has never known before.

I said earlier that there were no rivers to speak of in the inland suburbs, but this was not always so. 'Anyone who wishes to read and enjoy *The Lotos-eaters*', suggested one of Sydney's first literary journals, 'must put Mr Tennyson's volume in his pocket, and float – "falling asleep in a half dream" – up and down the Cook's River.' In those days the Cook's River district might indeed have passed for Tennyson's land of streams. Shea's Creek carried the purest water in Sydney, and the Mill Stream and the groundwater lakes of Botany were never dry. Cook's River itself lacked the downward smoke of Tennyson's waterfalls, but it used to wind its way prettily into Botany Bay between banks of green rushes.

All this has been changed by the process of compression. Shea's Creek has been turned into a canal, the groundwater lakes are surrounded by tanneries and evil-smelling wool scours, and Cook's River has lost almost all its charm. Its source is now dotted with the tombstones of Rookwood Cemetery, and its upper reaches are lined with concrete; from Canterbury racecourse it flows in its own bed through the respectable suburbs of Earlwood, Hurlstone Park, and Undercliffe, but farther downstream its bed has been rudely diverted to make way for a new runway at Kingsford Smith Airport. St Peters garbage tip nourishes seagulls and maggots near the junction of Cook's River and Shea's Creek, and often the air of this district is heavy with soot and ash from factories on the other side of the airport.

O'Riordan Street, the most direct route from the airport to the inner city, is undoubtedly the most noisome street in Sydney. Visitors arriving by air are thus obliged to run the fetid gauntlet of boiling-down works, fertiliser plants, and several other 'O' (Offensive) class industries. But who cares? Only the few people who still live in O'Riordan Street; Sydney as a whole is sublimely indifferent to the opinion of others.

'The smell from the galvaniser is the worst,' says one woman who has lived in O'Riordan Street for eighteen years. 'It gets in your throat. I think it must be acid or something. It's terrible noisy here too. Father works on night shift at the paper mill. He starts at eleven and works until seven o'clock in the morning. He comes home, and he's just getting off to sleep when the boilermakers over the road start work. They make a terrible lot of noise.' Half an hour later the first of the day's overseas jets taxis out to the runway on its ten enormous wheels. With the noise of a blizzard it hurtles across the filled-in corpse of Cook's River and rises steeply, trailing its black, downward smoke over Botany.

On the other side of the windshake, inland suburbia stretches out towards the belt of bush and rural land which is meant to contain the waves of expansion, but which has often been eroded instead. Long ago there used to be a wattle-tree in Panania that marked the highest point between East Hills and Central Station. The hillock upon which it grew was fifteen metres higher than the rest of the district, and the slopes were sparsely timbered with black-butt. In the early 1900s the trees disappeared to make way for orchards and ten-acre farms, and in 1931 the railway line reached East Hills, bringing with it a station called Panania – an Aboriginal word, so the Department of Railways explained, meaning 'The sun rising and shining on hills'. For the next fifteen years Panania was a suburb in name only. Then, in the late 1940s, a building boom began.

Some people came by choice, and some were sent by the Housing Commission. The difference is important, for it is now Panania's only form of class distinction; otherwise the Pananians are all pretty much on a level footing. The electoral roll starts with Ralph Abbott, duco-sprayer, and ends with Marija Zinkus, machinist. In between, there are fitters, toolmakers, cleaners, mail officers, glass workers, and wharf labourers. 'They were a bit militant about being workers at first, but not now,' says one of the local aldermen on Bankstown council. 'They still pride themselves on not being silvertails, though.'

In the 1960s Panania had a population of 10,000, but neither hotel nor sewer; seven schools, but scarcely any playing areas; sixty-two shops, but only one neon sign; a 'Personality' beauty salon, but no lending library. The Parents and Citizens' Association had been running a weekly dance for teenagers, but one night a gang of 'Rockers' closed the dance for good. Since then the only centres of nightlife had been the Star Theatre and the Miami milkbar. Panania has certainly risen, but it is not really shining yet. Other suns have risen far more spectacularly: notably Bankstown, Fairfield, Liverpool, Sutherland, and Blacktown.

Between Blacktown and Seven Hills, where Watkin Tench once walked in awful silence, the new suburb of Lalor Park has been needled into the face of Sydney like some gigantic tattoo. Each needle-prick is a fibro, timber or brick-veneer house built to Housing Commission specifications. 'It takes a bit of getting used to after Bondi,' says Mrs Marjorie Appleton, who has been living in Barbara Boulevarde for six months. 'I cried the first night I was up here, it was so lonely. I said, "This is a dead end." But it's better now there are more kids. When you can hear kids playing it's not such a wilderness!'

Goodness knows, Bondi has plenty of faults too. No trees shade its flats, for that would be a waste of the sunlight to which this suburb exposes itself so diligently. Its public rubbish bins all carry the legend, 'Skol for a Golden Sun Tan', and on a summer's day the glazed tile roofs between Bondi Junction and Dover Heights glisten as if every last one of them were oiled with 'Skol' or 'Vita-tan'. But Bondi is saved, of course, by its beach. Until their home was sold as part of a home-unit site, the Appletons used to live in Curlewis Street, only ten minutes' walk from the beach, and for their eighteen-year-old daughter Shirley this walk was a regular summer ritual. 'You sort of lose contact during the winter,' she says, 'and you more or less regain old friends in the summer. In winter you go around in couples, but in summer we all meet on the beach, and there are more parties, and the surf club has dances. It's beaut seeing everybody again at the beach, talking about what sort of costume you're going to get, and how the R. and R. team will do this season.'

Shirley's fiancé, a twenty-year-old electrician named Barry, spends four nights a week instructing Bondi's junior rescue and resuscitation team or training with the senior team. Every Saturday afternoon in the surfing season there is a carnival at one beach or another, and Bondi is always well represented. Shirley no longer goes to all the carnivals, but on Sundays she catches the train at Seven Hills and is on the beach with Barry by 9 am. They are joined there by other lifesavers and their girlfriends, but the boys seldom stay long. Barry and his mates have patrols to do, and they spend a good deal of time up on the clubhouse roof.

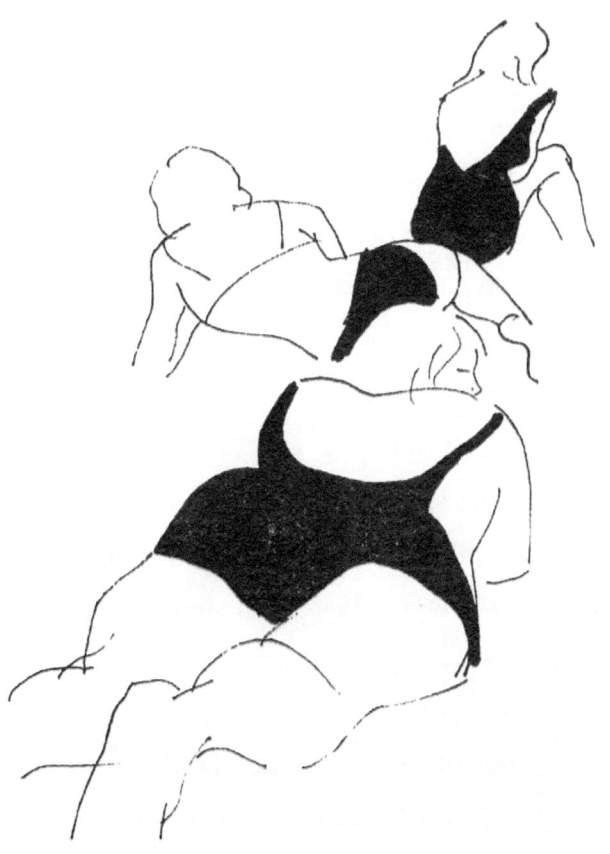

Shirley does not mind this separation. 'Beach boys are different from other boys,' she explains. 'A suburban boy might be more talkative and more polite, but beach boys are – I don't know – informal, I suppose you'd say.'

Shirley's parents miss the beach, but Stan Appleton finds that Lalor Park suits his job well: he is a debt collector, and there are plenty of hire-purchase defaulters in the great triangle bounded by Blacktown, Liverpool, and Bankstown. It is a hot Saturday morning, and Stan has a few calls to make at Yagoona. A tiny, leathery woman with henna'd hair answers his knock on the door; she is apologetic, but not in the least embarrassed. 'They was expecting an order for fridges, but it didn't come through, so they stood us all down. The aluminium company is going to ring me when they get some metal in. *He's* in Brisbane, as far as I know, and I'm out of work with the two kids.'

'Shot through, has he?' asks Stan sympathetically.

'He's a war neurosis case. I can show you the military pension book – twelve-pound-ten a fortnight. He's a good worker most of the time. Quiet around the house and that. But every three or four years he goes no-hoper. If he can bite a couple of quid he will. I just let him work his way out of it. When he comes home he has to start again from scratch. I try to clear things up for him. I'm paying five bob and ten bob at the door, but I got me own debts too.'

By midday the bitumen is bubbling, and pools of illusory water lie on the horizon of the Hume Highway; so Stan gives it away. In any case, he wants to get home in time to hear the first race. It's hot all right – no wind, not even a hot westerly; just dry, hot air that smites the eyes, vaporises petrol, and buckles railway lines. Out in the Paddock at Randwick punters are milling around the bookmakers' ring, soggy with perspiration but taut with excitement. 'Prices on the board,'

yell the bookies, 'give it a name! Prices on the board, give it a name!' Lalor's Glory, Bold Peter, Cabramatta Star, Lullaby Lass, Peace of Mind, Gay Gauntlet: which is the magic name? Runners dart about on their mysterious errands, obviously in possession of all the right names, and over at the rails a punter casually drops a bundle of fifty tenners into a bookmaker's bag, pockets his ticket, and strolls back into the members' stand.

During this interval between races, the stewards are holding an inquiry. 'I understand something happened near the six-furlong post and your rein broke,' says the chairman. The jockey is a vivid little figure in sweaty red and white silk. 'I eased in behind the two leaders,' he mutters, 'and the offside rein just give way and didn't give me much control.'

'Well, that's a rather remarkable thing. Did you pull him up?'

'No sir, I just eased him up and it just give away.'

'Did he interfere with any other horse?'

'No sir. Only King's Trial early in the race...'

There is no need for such suspicion as this at the Sydney Cricket Ground. Everything is above board there, and the only worry is the heat which presses down brutally on the Hill. The Hillites have only two comforts: the beer in their ice-boxes, and the occasional sense of relief afforded by the clean, hard sound of a batsman having a go.

The voice of the cricket commentator may be heard drowsily all over Sydney this Saturday afternoon, and race broadcasts come and go like pulses of delirium. At 8 o'clock the temperature drops to 30 degrees, but you'd never know it without a thermometer. The night air seems to have set like plaster, holding the silhouettes of a few gum trees rigid against the moonlit sky. Windows are open everywhere, but the curtains are perfectly still. At 9.30 am a southerly arrives at eighty kilometres an hour, with ice on its breath. You can hear it coming, banging doors in Sutherland, Panania, and Bankstown, filling the wind stockings at Mascot, ruffling the surface of Cook's River, scattering the garbage at St Peters and the betting tickets at Randwick and Warwick Farm, churning the plaster air, and lowering the temperature by ten degrees. It is as if the world had stopped for a few hours, and is now starting all over again.

The picture I have drawn of the inland suburbs is not a pleasant one, but I do not think I have been too harsh. Tench's desert is perfect for urban functions that require large areas of flat land – racing horses, burying the dead, slaughtering livestock, marshalling trains, building cheap houses. Most of these functions are necessary, but to my mind none of them is particularly engaging. Indeed, the only consolation I draw from the inland suburbs is that the farther one travels through them the closer one comes to the country. It is worth putting up with Bankstown and Fairfield in order to reach the lagoons near Windsor, where egrets wade among water lilies, or the open country around Campbelltown, tawny as a lion's flank.

There is little in Sydney to set one thinking about the country. The odour of greasy wool from a warehouse in Pyrmont may evoke half-forgotten memories, and so may the sound of a crow, or the sight of a swan flying high over the city. But these are only tenuous and casual reminders of a world with which the city was once intimately and manifestly connected, and from which – at least so far as appearances go – it is now almost divorced. In the early 1900s the country made its presence felt in the city. In those days Sydney owed most of its prosperity to primary industries, and every second person in the city seemed to have relatives in the country. No longer is this the case. Sydney now has a larger population than the rest of New South Wales put together, and when country cousins come down to the city they are liable to become lost in the crowd. Secondary and tertiary industries have stolen much of the country's limelight, and family connections have grown weaker year by year.

Yet the estrangement is not quite complete. Once a year, at the Royal Easter Show, city and country come together for a lavish, boisterous family reunion. Down comes the country, with the best it has to offer: winesap and Jonathan apples from Glen Innes, pumpkins from Wagga, comeback wool from Boggabri, preserved fruit from the Riverina, Poll Herefords from Uralla, steer-riders and bulldoggers from Tenterfield, woodchoppers from Wauchope and Kyogle. The city responds with new cars and tractors, forged steel axes, television sets and refrigerators, potato chips, kewpie dolls, Jimmy Sharman's boxing tent, Delilah Jones and Her Fabulous Hotcha Show.

Over at the woodchop arena, competitors in white trousers, singlets and blazers sit beneath the grandstand sharpening their axes, caressing the sides of the blades with oilstone, and stropping them with the palms of their hands. The blades are already as sharp as they will ever be, but their owners keep on sharpening automatically – sharpening, and talking to one another in somewhat guarded fashion. One of them tests his blade on a log, chiselling the log as if it were balsa. 'Too hard, this wood,' he mutters.

'Too bloody hard,' agrees a man in a North Coast blazer who is passing his right palm in a circular movement over his axehead. 'I helped cut these blocks near Port Macquarie. We cut them four weeks ago last Monday and lorried them in to the railway. There's been no rain, and they been in the sun all that time. Makes it tough for a man. It's not a race, it's an endurance test!'

Another competitor enters the yard, takes an axe from its case, and sits down beside the man in the North Coast blazer. 'I seen you roaring down Pacific Highway the other day,' he remarks in mock-aggressive tone. 'Too bloody proud to wave!'

The North Coast man stops rubbing his axe. 'What day?' he asks, not sure just how serious the accusation might be.

'Wednesday.'

'That'd be me.'

'A green ute?'

'That's right. I didn't see you, mate.'

On the far side of the Showground, opposite the woodchop arena in mood as well as place, the sideshow spruikers are lifting their voices in hoarse cacophony. 'Ooh, la, la, la; Greta and Gretel, the Unbelievable Twins! One headless and one legless! They're real, they're alive, they're amazing! If you're not broad-minded when you come in, you'll be broad-minded when you come out!' The voices of city and country rise and mingle everywhere. 'Ooh, la, la, la, la!

There's ghosts in here! By golly jingo, you go in one door and you run out the other!'... 'He should develop into a really good bull; he has a good heart, but on closer inspection that frame is really rather loose, and I'd like to let it go for another twelve months and see what it's like then'... 'Watch your marks, axemen! All right axemen, stand to your blocks! Get ready! One, two, three, four, five, six...'... 'I say, this is where you get your chicken rolls. Yes sir! I say, this is where you get a nice hot cup of tea and a beautiful chicken roll!'... 'It's a progressive town, Crookwell. Six stock and station agents and four hotels. And clean; that's the main thing. It's a real clean little district...'

Horsemen ride beside motorcyclists, tractors are offered for sale beside sports cars, cattle are driven through the crowd on their way to the arena, and the smell of animal dung unites with those of cooking fat, diesel oil, beer, fairy floss, meat pies, cut flowers, and fresh fruit. It is all most unnatural, but for this little while, in this small space, city and country are one.

6

'THE NORTH SHORE,' wrote one of its most assiduous historians, the late Charles Whitham, 'was so called from the very early days because – well, what else could you call it, if you stood at Sydney Cove and looked across to the opposing coast?' I suppose we may count ourselves lucky that it was not called "The Opposing Coast". Sydney has never been much of a hand at name giving, and as settlement spread across the harbour the usual easy mixture of distinguished English personal names and euphonious Aboriginal place names was applied to the wilderness bounded by Port Jackson and the Lane Cove River, the northern beaches, and Broken Bay. For some obscure reason the whole of this region became known as the Hundred of Packenham. I have never been able to discover who or what the original Packenham may have been, but in any case the division of the County of Cumberland into Hundreds was never of much practical significance. What did provide the northern region with clear and durable identity was the division of Packenham into seven municipalities and one shire: North Sydney, Mosman, Willoughby, Manly, Lane Cove, Hunter's Hill, Kuring-gai, and Warringah.

Nothing could be less like the desert from which we have just emerged. Inland suburbia sprawls across a flat shale plain, while the North Shore takes its shape from the ridges, valleys, and foreshores of a sandstone plateau; the one possesses neither bush nor sea, the other is blessed with both. 'If the country were rolled out flat it would be very much larger,' wrote the literal-minded Charles Whitham. 'Nowhere is it level, and nowhere are you more than five miles from water. Of its 170,000 acres about 15,000 are covered by the lake-like expanses of Pittwater, Lane Cove, Middle Harbour and Cowan Creek.'

As more names were applied to these parts, and particularly after the opening of the North Shore railway line in the 1890s, the term 'North Shore' acquired a new and narrower meaning. To outsiders it continued to mean everything north of the harbour, but gradually those who lived there themselves came to realise that the North Shore was something considerably less than the Hundred of Packenham. It was, and is, an area between the Lane Cove River and Middle Harbour Creek. It ends at Wahroonga; there can be no doubt about that. But precisely where it begins – Chatswood, Roseville, Lindfield? – is anyone's guess.

Perhaps the most sensible starting point would be Boundary Road, where Willoughby gives way to Kuring-gai, for in most respects the North Shore is now synonymous with the Municipality of Kuring-gai. In this narrower manifestation it is removed from the sea, yet still pervaded by the bush, and this suits it down to the ground. If the North Shore had to choose between the two elements representing change and permanence, it would surely plump for permanence. I shall have more to say about this later, but first I must describe the railway line that divides the North Shore right down its middle.

A good train to catch in the evening is the 5.17 from Wynyard, which runs non-stop through Wollstonecraft, St Leonards and Artarmon. Roseville and Lindfield are also subliminal images glimpsed from the corner of the eye – first a blur of purple lantana, then a pastiche of chrome and duco on the Pacific Highway. From Killara onwards, the train stops every three minutes: Gordon, Pymble, Turramurra, Warrawee, Wahroonga...No need to lift one's eyes from the evening paper; some inner clockwork warns each traveller when his time has come.

At every station thirty or forty leave the train, fumble for their tickets, and ascend the steps together. As each traveller reaches the overhead bridge he or she must turn either east or west, and it is here that the unity of the train journey ends and the dichotomy of the North Shore reasserts itself.

Those who turn west go steeply down roads like Bushlands Avenue, Kissing Point Road or Fox Valley Road, and turn into streets which only a few years ago were bush. The bush may have been pushed aside, but it is never very far away; it arches overhead, dropping gum leaves onto the skillion roofs of Warragul and Waratah roads, and it besieges the back fences of the newer homes. Given half a chance, it will come right inside.

One night in Turramurra I was awakened at 3 am by the sound of a poker falling on the hearth of the fireplace. Our cat was outside, I remembered, so I got up and switched on the sitting-room light. The room seemed empty, but the carpet in front of the fireplace was covered with soot. Then out from behind the sofa walked a small grey creature with a long bushy tail. Although I had never seen a possum at close quarters before, I knew that this was one, and that it had tumbled down the chimney.

The bush does not always intrude as abruptly as this, but on the western side of the line one is constantly aware of its presence. Kookaburras perch on the rotary hoist, bandicoots dig for grubs in the lawn, and there is always the unnerving possibility that a funnel-web spider may sidle under the back door and take up residence in someone's slipper. This last thought is enough to make the shaking of shoes and slippers second nature. It is not that the funnel-web actually does much harm; in recent years very few deaths have been attributed to its venom in Sydney, and many of its victims have recovered from their bites, but as an object of suburban dread nothing else from the bush can match the waddling, hairy-legged *Atrax robustus*. Because of the way its fangs are placed, the funnel-web can bite only by rearing back on its hind legs and striking downwards – a posture and movement which create a picture of unbridled ferocity. Within ten minutes of that downward strike, the victim turns pale, feels weak and ill, and starts to perspire. Within twelve hours the victim may be dead.

No one I know has ever been bitten by a funnel-web, but one of my neighbours once found a colony of twenty-five in the roots of a tree he had chopped down, and an old man of my acquaintance tells a hair-raising story of the time when he lived as a hermit in a North Shore cave. One night he woke up to feel something crawling across his face; he brushed it off, and went stoically back to sleep. Next morning he found a drowned funnel-web floating in the tumbler of water where he kept his false teeth. Either it had been brushed straight into the tumbler, or it had later climbed over the ledge beside his bed and fallen from there into the jaws of death.

Whenever I think of the bush I think of it in summer, when it is most alive. Blue-tongue lizards wake from their winter sleep, wildflowers unfold, and cicadas claw their way out of the earth to sing for a few weeks in the sun. For every week the cicada spends in sunlight, it has probably spent a year in the dark. Before she dies, the female cicada forces eggs into the bark of a tree. The young cicada, no larger than a flea, falls to the ground and digs its way down to the roots of the tree. For five years or so it sucks the sap in this unimaginable dungeon, growing into a brown nymph not unlike a lobster in shape, but no more than a few centimetres long. Then it burrows up towards the light.

Whatever instinct may have brought the cicada nymph to the surface now persuades it to climb a tree trunk, dig its claws into the bark, and escape from its mud-stained shell. The shell splits between the shoulders, and gradually the cicada's soft, spongy body forces its way through the opening. It is shrivelled and misshapen at first, but already the sunlight is hardening its tissues. Within an hour its steel-rimmed gauze wings are dry and straight, its armoured body-plates are hard, its helmet-like head is round and smooth, and its kettle-drums are taut. It is ready to sing.

By mid-November the tree trunks are dotted with empty suits of armour, and up in the branches, wings glistening in the sun, a host of Yellow Mondays, Green Grocers, and Black Princes contract and release the membranes of their drums. The clicking becomes faster, louder and shriller until every last tree in the bush seems to be chanting a feverish, deafening hymn to the sun.

All too soon, these singers are silenced by the sparrow's beak, the sugar-glider's teeth or, most horrible of all, the sand wasp's sting. The black and orange sand wasp drives its sting into the cicada's body, causing instant paralysis, but not death. Hunter and prey fall to the ground together, and the wasp tugs the cicada over the bush floor and into its burrow. It then lays an egg on its victim's belly and the cicada lies there blind and dumb, waiting to be eaten.

The sunlight that hardens the cicadas' wings, tightens their membranes, and moves them to song also dries the coarse bush grass and encourages leaf litter in the bush to release its volatile oils into the stifling summer air. Eucalyptus oils have a low flashpoint, and there are times when the air in the bush is almost as inflammable as the leaves on the ground. Combine this with low humidity, high winds, and a smouldering cigarette, and you have all the makings of a bushfire.

I remember one particular January day well. There had been a few fires the day before, and from the train window in the morning I could see a bluish haze in the bush. By 11 am the westerly was blowing smoke across the Pacific Highway near Cowan, and driving a fire straight up from the valley. There were really two fires: one burning steadily through the undergrowth, another leaping half a mile ahead through the trees. At about 11.15 am the treetop fire jumped the highway.

A Catholic priest driving north from Cowan stopped his car when he saw some dull orange flames through the smoke ahead. By all that was sensible he should have turned around and driven back to Cowan; instead he got out of the car and ran *into* the smoke and flames. 'Don't ask me why,' he said later. 'When I saw the flames coming, I just jumped out of the car and ran.'

At least he had the sense to remove his celluloid collar, and wrap his black coat around his head. Peering through the lapels he ran along the highway, headfirst into the back of a car parked in temporary safety between two walls of flame. Two men sitting in the car refused to leave it, so he ran on alone until he reached a roadside café. By then he had second- and third-degree burns on his face and neck, and second-degree burns on both hands. All this happened on one of the city's main highways.

Later in the day another fire broke out in Lane Cove National Park, burning a few back fences and blowing hot ash onto back verandahs. From my train window that evening the fire looked like a city that had sprung suddenly from the bush, dotting the twilight with lighted windows, street lamps, and neon signs; but all the lights were orange. The bush along Lane Cove River seemed strangely inhabited, yet in reality it had never been more deserted. Most of its creatures would have fled from the fire, and even the cicada nymphs must have stirred uneasily as the furnace roared overhead.

The eastern side of the North Shore line has its bushfires, too, but over there the bush is not quite so intrusive. If one keeps driving east along Mona Vale Road or Bobbin Head Road, one will eventually come to places like Eucalyptus Road, St Ives, or Warrimoo Road, North Turramurra, and these have much in common with the bushy streets running off Ryde Road, Kissing Point Road and Fox Valley Road: their houses are relatively new and well kept, and sometimes in the dead of night possums fall into their sitting-rooms, too. Septic tanks stand in their backyards like tombs, or hide discreetly under *Monstera deliciosa*, and the Progress Association, which meets once a month, has much to talk about. These similarities demonstrate the futility of making absolute comparisons between the 'right' and the 'wrong' sides of the line, yet there is no blinking the fact that parts of the eastern side – not such parvenus as St Ives or North Turramurra, but the rich, juicy neighbourhoods closer in to the line – are, to use the haughty real-estate term, 'preferred'. 'The people who live in Kuring-gai,' wrote Charles Whitham in 1927, 'think they are very much better than the worst. Asparagus and olives are ordinary comestibles, some of them dress for dinner, and the vulgar Australian habit of drinking tea at meals is regarded as *contra bonos mores*.' Things have changed a lot since then, but many of the people in Kuring-gai still consider themselves very much better than the worst, and there are now more streets than ever in which not only are asparagus and olives ordinary comestibles but also Jaguars and Daimlers are ordinary conveyances, Boxers and Borzois are ordinary dogs, jacarandas and Illawarra flames are ordinary trees, directorships are ordinary jobs, and Shore and Abbotsleigh are ordinary schools.

Sydney may not be as class-conscious as some other cities, but if it has no rigid classes it has plenty of classifications. 'The distinctions in society here remind me of the "Dockyard people" described by Dickens, that keen and kindly satirist of modern follies,' wrote Mrs Charles Meredith in the late 1830s in her *Notes and Sketches of New South Wales*. 'Thus – Government officers don't know merchants; merchants with "stores" don't know other merchants who keep "shops"; and the shopkeepers have, I doubt not, a little code of their own, prescribing the proper distance to be observed between drapers and haberdashers, butchers and pastry cooks.' If you think we have outgrown such silliness, I would refer you to a sociological survey by the University of New South Wales (*Status Ranking of Occupations in Sydney*) which graded 135 separate occupations. The five most 'preferred' classifications were doctors, university professors, solicitors, company directors and architects; and down at the bottom of the ladder were wharf labourers, barmaids, seasonal labourers, charwomen, unskilled labourers, and road sweepers. No one would suggest that each of these status groups keeps its inferiors at arm's length, but the different degrees of status attaching to each occupation undoubtedly combine with such other determinants as income, education and address to maintain the fairly sturdy social barriers that lie beneath the egalitarian surface of Sydney. Mrs Marcel Dekyvere, who is married to a wool buyer from Darling Point, maintains that the members of her socially powerful Black and White Ball Committee are drawn from a wide variety of suburbs and occupations. So they may be, but needless to say none of them is married to a butcher from Crow's Nest or a commercial traveller from Burwood.

Although it is most unlikely that any two people would agree on the order of all 367 suburbs listed in another late 1960s survey by the University of New South Wales (*Status Ranking of Sydney Suburbs*), there would probably be substantial agreement on the selection, if not the grading, of the first twenty or so. According to the survey, and in order of rank, the most 'preferred' suburbs are Vaucluse, Point Piper, Darling Point, Bellevue Hill, Pymble, Palm Beach, Potts Point, Killara, Wahroonga, Beauty Point, Castlecrag, Elizabeth Bay, Dover Heights, Rose Bay, Clifton Gardens, Double Bay, Roseville, Roseville Chase, Turramurra, and Clontarf. Although the first four places go to the purplest of the eastern suburbs, the northern suburbs on this short list outnumber their eastern rivals by eleven to nine. And of the eleven, six are in Kuring-gai.

The foremost of these six are undoubtedly Pymble, Killara, and Wahroonga; but despite the survey, I feel that Killara has a slight edge on the other two. Don't ask me why: somehow the Abbotsleigh uniforms seem greener in Killara, the textured brick a deeper red, the jacarandas more luminously mauve. At the time of writing, its residents included the Mayor of Kuring-gai, both State and Federal Members of Parliament for the upper North Shore, the editor of *The Sydney Morning Herald*, the secretary of the Linnean Society, and the chairman of the Australian Meat Board. The electoral roll included two professors, three judges, fourteen stockbrokers, 26 manufacturers, 58 doctors, 66 lawyers, 99 managers and no fewer than 178 company directors. Admittedly Killara also has one of the only two hotels in Kuring-gai, but the Greengate is safely over on the western side of the line, and in any case it is by far one of the most venerable-looking hotels in Sydney.

What name could be more apt than Killara, an Aboriginal word meaning 'permanent' or 'always there'? The big pseudo-Tudor houses called Oak Lodge or Rochester or Tavistock seem as durable and dependable as the metal railway tickets on their owners' keyrings. The owners themselves may not be absolutely permanent, but most of Killara's residents remain there a long, long time. The postman, Mr R. Burke, has been living and working in Killara since 1923. There were only 418 houses on his run then; forty years later there were 2400.

In spite of this increase, Killara has preserved its early character pretty much intact. Its standard of living is still affluent, its politics are still conservative (at the 1961 Federal election it cast only 247 votes for the Labor Party), and its religion is still staunchly Protestant. 'You never see any Catholic school uniforms at the station,' says one resident. The remark expresses neither approval nor disapproval; it is merely a statement of fact. The late Reverend Leo Charlton was rector of St Martin's Church of England for forty years.

'He'd meet me on my rounds,' recalls Mr Burke, 'and he'd say, "What's new, Burky? Who's new in Stanhope Road?" I'd tell him, and he'd write it down on his cigarette packet. "He's no good to you," I'd say. "He's not a cash customer." "Listen, Burky," he'd say, "if he comes to my church and listens to my sermon, he changes his spots overnight!"'

Killara seldom becomes angry, for most of the time there is little to anger it, but any threat to its integrity can move the suburb to passionate self-defence. The last time this happened was when the suggestion came up that Kuring-gai Council Chambers should be moved from Gordon to Killara. Killara? Five hundred people packed the Memorial Hall. It was the biggest protest meeting since the days of Jack Lang, and the liveliest, too. Before the evening was over, one Kuring-gai alderman had said to another, in a voice that could be heard clearly all over the hall: 'I beg your pardon, sir! Did you call me a bastard?'

You could have heard a pin drop. An accusation of this kind on the platform at a public meeting in Killara was as utterly unexpected and discordant as, to take an earlier local example, the unsolved strangling of a housewife in Northcote Avenue. A friend of mine who lives in Wattle Street, only a block away from Northcote Avenue, went to the Korean War a few days after that murder was committed, and on his first day in Seoul he found himself talking to a soldier from Sydney. 'Have you heard about the murder in Killara?' he asked. 'Murder in Killara?' exclaimed the soldier, aghast. 'Oh, no!'

Amid the uncertainties of war in Asia, it must indeed have seemed as if Sydney's certainties were crumbling too, as if security were giving way to hazard, and permanence to change. *A murder in Killara? Oh, no!*

7

NO ONE really knows Sydney who has not seen it from the immense body of water that ebbs and flows between the Heads, runs past the city and under the bridge to Parramatta, spills into North Harbour and Middle Harbour, and all in all invades more than seventy bays and coves. This is because the harbour both adorns and reveals: it has the power to lift one's heart, so suddenly and magnificently does it come into view, and it has the power to reveal aspects of the city that are visible only from water level.

My favourite view is from the lookout near Taronga Park Zoo. There are some low bushes to be pushed through first, a few ledges of sandstone to be climbed, and all at once I see the harbour extending from Rose Bay to the bridge, and back past the crowded hillsides of Kirribilli and Cremorne to Bradley's Head, thick with bush and shrill with cicadas. Two Manly ferries pass each other near Clark Island, a Mosman ferry is rounding Cremorne Point, and a hundred scattered sails are leaning away from the wind. From this distance the harbour looks blue, but at close quarters, even on perfectly clear days, it is dark green, as if still coloured by the bush that grew upon its bed half a million years ago.

Somewhere in the zoo a lion roars, disturbing herds of comfy bungalows on the slopes of Mosman. On still nights a roar like that can be heard in Woollahra. Sound travels a long way across water, and there are nights when one can stand on the beach at Balmoral and hear the lonely clanging of a junction buoy as it rides the swell where eastern and western channels come together in the main harbour.

Just as the harbour continually surprises one upon land, so the land sometimes comes as a surprise upon the harbour. Empty gun emplacements cling to the cliffs of Middle Head, unseen except from the water, and secluded beaches – Milk Beach, Kutti Beach, Obelisk Beach, Collins Beach – glisten secretly between water and bush. The bush behind Collins Beach, near Manly, is as dense today as it was when Governor Phillip landed there in 1790, and was speared through the right shoulder. 'The Governor attempted to run,' recorded one of his companions, Lieutenant Henry Waterhouse, 'holding the spear with both hands to keep the end off the ground, but, owing to the length, the end took the ground and stopped him short (I suppose it could not be less than 12 feet long). He then beged me for God's sake to haul the spear out, which I immediatly stoped to do and was in the act of doing it, when I recollected I should only haul the barb into his flesh again which was an inch long. I then determined on breaking it off and bent it down for that purpose, but owing to its length could not effect it. I then bent it upwards but could not break it owing to the toughness of the wood. Just at this instant another spear came and just grazed the skin off between the thumb and forefinger of my right hand. I must own it frightened me a good deal and I believe added to my exertions; for the next sudden jerk I gave it broke short off...'

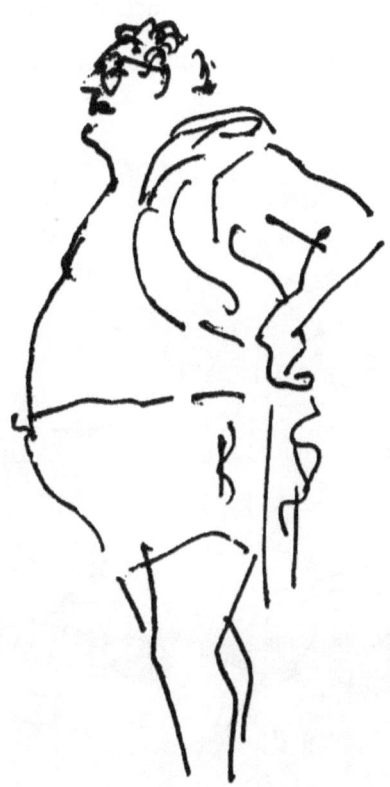

The scene is more peaceful here today. Several yachts and motor cruisers are moored a few yards from shore, and their crews and passengers are picnicking on the sand. A young underwater fisherman walks ashore with an octopus impaled on the end of his hand spear; the spear looks about as long as the one that hung down from Phillip's shoulder, but instead of a barb it has a prong. He removes the octopus, chases his shrieking girlfriend up the beach with it, and then callously rubs it on her bare back. She screams in earnest now, and the picnic crowd mutters disapprovingly.

There is much to be seen around the shoreline of the main harbour. The headquarters of the Australian Security Intelligence Organisation lurks behind a big house in Kirribilli, invisible from the street but quite visible from the harbour, and nearby the gardens of Kirribilli House (the Prime Minister's Sydney residence) and Admiralty House (the Governor-General's) stand exposed to the idle gaze of ferry travellers and Lascar seamen. Only from the harbour, too, can one see the vast and thunderous belly of the Harbour Bridge, the pines and aloes of Clark Island, and some of the old stone mansions and new glass towers of Darling Point.

The eastern side of Darling Point is dominated by Carthona, a delightful Gothic house built a few feet above the harbour by Sir Thomas Mitchell in the 1830s, while the western side is dominated by the glass and concrete cliff of Yarranabbe Gardens. These are the two contending motifs of the harbour side eastern suburbs – the stately sandstone house set in an acre or two of lawn and leafy shade, and the luxurious block of home units. Nowhere are they statelier or more luxurious than on Darling Point.

Between the 1830s and 1870s, some of Sydney's wealthiest families settled on this point. 'There are certain spots two or three miles out of town,' wrote Anthony Trollope in 1872, 'now occupied generally by villas and included in the grounds of some happy resident, which leave nothing for the imagination to add. Greenoaks and Mount Adelaide, belonging to two brothers, Mr Thomas and Mr Henry Mort, are perfect.

Sir James Martin, who was Prime Minister when I was first there, and who I hope may soon be so again, has a garden falling down to the sea, which is like fairyland.' The Knoxes built Fiona, the Horderns built Retford Hall, and the Tooths built The Swifts. Bellevue Hill and Vaucluse may have their own particular cachets compounded of social exclusiveness and vertiginously high unimproved capital values, but they can never match the aura of prosperous tranquillity that emanates from a pair of wrought-iron gates and a red gravel drive on Darling Point.

There is nothing quite so prosperous-looking anywhere else in Sydney, and the only comparable air of tranquillity is perhaps to be found at Hunter's Hill. During the 1840s two French brothers, Didier and Jules Joubert, bought 200 acres of land on the peninsula between the Lane Cove and Parramatta rivers, imported seventy stonemasons from Lombardy, and began building sandstone houses of great permanence and charm. One of the first of these, St Malo, has had to be moved from the path of a new highway, but Passy and other old houses remain undisturbed in a sequestered calm.

The old homes of the eastern suburbs have been less successful in preserving their original character: The Hermitage was bought by Woolworths as a staff training college; the Archbishop lives at Green oaks and, as if to restore the balance, the Cardinal has moved into The Swifts; Rona and Kambala have been turned into girls' schools; Redleaf has become Woollahra Council Chambers; and Retford Hall has been knocked down to make room for a twenty-storey home-unit block called Thornton Place.

On Darling Point, Potts Point, Macleay Point and Blues Point, in Kirribilli, Neutral Bay, Cremorne, and Mosman, the construction of home-unit blocks has radically altered the appearance of the slopes and foreshores of the main harbour. Mosman, once so utterly settled in its ways, is becoming virtually a new suburb. By the time this suburb started growing in the nineteenth century, the whalers had left Mosman's Bay; just as well too, for Mosman could never have tolerated anything as rowdy and smelly as a whaling station. Such dubious elements as artists' camps and Chinese flax farms were squeezed out, and by 1930 the place had acquired an air of placid contentment.

For the next two decades Mosman seemed to be maintaining its enviable status quo; in reality its population was slowly declining and its houses were deteriorating. It had more old people, and a lower proportion of males to females, than any other municipality in Sydney. Then, in the late 1950s, a process of renewal began. Speculators and homeowners renovated individual houses, but the most important midwives at the rebirth of Mosman were the high-density developers who bought two or three old properties, demolished them, amalgamated their titles, and threw up blocks of twenty or thirty units, all with harbour views. Home units craned their necks from every ridge, and down at Balmoral the marble temple built in expectation of a Second Coming was replaced by a whole village under one roof.

It seems only natural that the shores of the harbour should be undergoing some sort of transformation, for the harbour itself exists in a continual state of change. The Heads through which the new Messiah was once expected to come have indeed admitted strange visitors: convict transports and ships of war, ships from Egypt and Turkey, Iceland and the Argentine, sharks, sea leopards, whales, and stingarees. I once saw something swimming near Middle Head that looked like a cormorant. It turned out to be a fairy penguin.

The tides rise and fall about five feet each day, covering and uncovering the Sow and Pigs reef near junction buoy, and swirling into a dangerous bombora off Dobroyd Point. A naval surveyor named John Gowlland was drowned in 1874 while taking soundings over this bombora; the sea looked calm enough to Gowlland and his crew, but suddenly a big wave rose out of nowhere and swamped their rowing boat. Some leadlines fouled on the harbour bed, holding the boat upside down, and Commander Gowlland was drowned while swimming towards shore.

The most sudden change of all on the harbour occurs when a southerly buster meets an incoming tide. Towards the end of a very hot day with only a light westerly, or perhaps no wind at all, a southerly may come roaring across Sydney at up to one hundred kilometres an hour. A great cloud of dust appears over the eastern suburbs, and a minute or two later the southerly hits the harbour, whipping it into surf and capsizing small boats. Sydney's pioneer newspaper editor, Robert Howe, was drowned in 1829 when his fishing boat was overturned in this fashion near Pinchgut.

Pinchgut has seen some changes, too. In the early years of the colony this rocky little island was used as a place of confinement and punishment for recalcitrant convicts. Later, during the Russian scare of the 1840s and 1850s, it was razed almost to sea level and fortified with a sandstone Martello tower. 'You laugh, and with reason, at the panic which led people in these colonies to insist upon fortifying themselves against the Russians,' wrote Sir William Denison, the Governor after whom the new fort was named. 'I never partook of this panic, but I have gone into the question of the defence of Sydney for the purpose of keeping off much more unpleasant neighbours than the Russians; namely our friends the French and our relations the Americans. The access to this harbour is so easy that unless we have some batteries ready to open upon vessels lying off the town, a few frigates might run in under cover of the night, and the first notice I should have of their arrival would be a 32-pound shot crashing through the walls of my house.'

Some years earlier two American frigates had in fact entered the harbour at night. 'Had war existed,' the American Commodore remarked cheerily next day, 'we might, after firing the shipping, and reducing the great part of the town to ashes, have effected a retreat before daybreak in perfect safety.' Strangely enough, the only time Fort Denison ever came under fire was from an American cruiser, the USS *Chicago*.

Fort Denison had been conceived as the central point of an inner defence ring consisting of batteries at Dawes Point, Kirribilli, Mrs Macquarie's Chair, and Fort Macquarie, but no sooner had it been completed than this inner ring was superseded by an outer ring of batteries on Bradley's Head, Middle Head, George's Head, and South Head. Nowadays Fort Denison does little more than record the tide and ring a fog bell, though up in its tower three well-kept cannon still stare through their embrasures at the frigates that never came. When danger did come, a century later than expected, there was absolutely nothing Fort Denison could do about it.

This danger began on the night of 29 May 1942, when a tiny seaplane launched from the Japanese submarine I.21 flew through the Heads at an altitude of only 180 metres. An observer sketched openings in Sydney's anti-submarine boom, and noted the positions of 'a battleship, cruiser and other units' near Garden Island. After flying undetected over the bridge, the plane turned back to sea and landed beside its submarine. The I.21 was then joined by three more submarines, and at 4.30 pm on 31 May each of the four launched a midget submarine carrying two torpedoes and a crew of two officers. Like sharks or sea leopards, these vessels glided through the Heads and searched out the gaps in the boom.

Gavin Souter

They were detected at about 10 pm, and a general alarm was sent out to all ships in the harbour. At 10.35 pm one midget submarine, which had become enmeshed in the boom, was exploded by its own crew, and at 10.57 pm the USS *Chicago* began firing five-inch shells at the conning tower of another midget which had been picked up by searchlights. One of these shells ricocheted off the water and hit the tower at Fort Denison, cracking one of the granite joggles that bind its blocks of sandstone together.

Half an hour after midnight, one of the invaders fired its two torpedoes – the only ones fired that night – from a position near Bradley's Head. Both were aimed at the *Chicago*. One missed the cruiser by three metres and sank a naval ferry at Garden Island, killing twenty-two sailors who were asleep onboard. The other ran ashore without exploding.

When the sun came up next morning, three patrol boats were battering the last midget submarine to pieces in Taylor's Bay. This was not quite the end. Six nights later one of the mother submarines surfaced off the Heads and sent ten shells flying into the eastern suburbs. Most of them failed to explode, and there were in fact only two casualties: a young woman was cut on the elbow by flying glass, and a man broke one of his ankles jumping out of bed when a dead shell tore through the wall of his bedroom.

These were slight scars, but memorable ones. The last time I was out on the harbour we sailed into Taylor's Bay, calm in its little crescent of bush, and then made around Bradley's Head towards the city. It was Saturday afternoon, and four or five hundred other yachts were bobbing and heeling in all directions, their spinnakers of coloured nylon billowing as they ran before the nor'-easter, and their white mainsails flapping and cracking like gunfire as they made about. People were standing all over the HMAS *Sydney* mast on Bradley's Head watching a line of eighteen-footers race down the western channel, and as we passed I heard a familiar sound – not the cicada song that had once welcomed me home to this supremely beautiful harbour, but the shrill chanting of Randwick. Even war memorials unbend a little on Saturday afternoon.

It may seem strange that the sinking of a German raider in the Indian Ocean should have a memorial on Bradley's Head while the sinking of a Japanese raider near this very spot has none. Yet really Taylor's Bay needs no memorial: there is no chance of our ever forgetting the night the submarines got in, for that was when we realised, vaguely but inescapably, that there were sand wasps in the world.

www.ingramcontent.com/pod-product-compliance
Lightning Source LLC
Chambersburg PA
CBHW021356300426
44114CB00012B/1258